SECRET VINEYARDS
·OF FRANCE·

Secret Vineyards
· OF FRANCE ·

Christine Atkinson

Colour photographs by
FRED ATKINSON

DAVID & CHARLES
Newton Abbot   London
HIPPOCRENE BOOKS INC
New York

To all the friendly and dedicated *vignerons* whose help has been invaluable and whose wine is delightful.

ACKNOWLEDGEMENTS

Special thanks are due to my husband for all the photographs which appear in this book, and for his unending patience and encouragement. I also owe an enormous debt of gratitude to my good friend Colin Crowfoot for his meticulous help in preparing the maps and the happy times we had whilst working together on them.

Thanks are equally due to Judith, Colin's wife, who has helped in so many intangible ways and double-checked my proof-reading.

(*page 2*) Secret vineyards . . . where no main roads pass by and few tourists penetrate

Maps by Ethan Danielson

British Library Cataloguing in Publication Data

Atkinson, Christine
  Secret vineyards of France.
  1. Viticulture——France
  I. Title
  944'.083'7   SB387.8.F8

ISBN 0-7153-9118-6 (Great Britain)

Typeset by ABM Typographics Limited Hull
Printed in Italy
by New Interlitho, S.p.A. Milan
for David & Charles Publishers plc
Brunel House   Newton Abbot   Devon

Published in the United States of America
by Hippocrene Books Inc
171 Madison Avenue, New York, NY10016

CONTENTS

(*Overleaf main picture*) The rock of Solutré, famous landmark of the Pouilly-Fuissé area. (*Inset top to bottom*) Katie working in the Rochefort vineyards. Not only does the harvest demand teams of workers – here several men are needed to do the *effeuillage* work, removing unwanted suckers from the plants. Your guide will use a pipette to draw up the wine from the barrel . . .

Part One
DISCOVERING FRENCH WINE

WINES AT SOURCE

Wine has always been associated with romance and to most of us the differing tastes to be experienced are something of a voyage of discovery. The past few years have witnessed a surge of interest in the subject of wine and our consumption of it rises annually. This interest is no longer confined to people with large bank accounts, nor to an élite group of connoisseurs. People are drinking wine simply because they enjoy it, not because it is the fashionable thing to do, and they are people from every age and income bracket.

Those of us who live in non wine-producing countries however, unless we travel abroad regularly, tend to have only a limited experience of wine. A Frenchman has an innate knowledge of it because it is part of his heritage; even the French of Normandy, one of the *départements* not producing wine, will be accustomed to drinking it as part of the daily routine, and will recognise the difference between the *vin de table* which accompanies their meals and those other bottles reserved for special occasions.

Holidays apart, most of us find our wine in restaurants, wine shops or on the shelves of the supermarkets. Although it is fair to say that many of our restaurants and hotels are now trying to offer a more interesting selection on their wine menu, for economic reasons most of them can only afford to stock a modest cellar and so aim to please the average customer's taste. A discerning customer is therefore likely to be disappointed.

Many of our wine shops have begun to stock their shelves far more imaginatively and yet their moderately priced wines are only a pale reflection of the pure wines available in the country of origin. It is a well-known fact that what is imported in vast quantities to satisfy the general demand is usually wine from inferior areas of a wine growing region, or simply a blend of several widely differing wines made up by a shipper who knows that if the price is reasonable, and the label has a well-known name on it, such as Bordeaux or Burgundy, the vast majority of us will buy it and find it acceptable. The reason, of course, is that, if we have never had the opportunity to taste the 'real' wine bearing that label, we have nothing to compare it with.

When the more interesting wines *are* to be found in the wine shops they usually have such a high price ticket on them that they are beyond our reach, except for those special occasions when we persuade ourselves that it is worth the extravagance. As for finding such wines in restaurants and hotels, one only has to compare the price of the same bottle in the shop to lose most of one's enthusiasm for ordering it. 'Overheads' have a great deal to answer for.

The supermarkets have played an important part in bringing wine into the weekly shopping basket, and through their buyers' selections and their competitive promotion campaigns they have helped to arouse the current interest.

However, one can see two distinct elements involved in wine consumption. At one end of the scale there is much snobbery, possibly to do with the history of wine. In the eighteenth and nineteenth centuries wine was drunk only by the upper classes, much of it the highly favoured claret, or Bordeaux. The twentieth century has seen great advances in wine technology, with the result that the lesser wines have improved vastly in quality, leading to more good wines being increasingly available to all, not just to the wealthy. The snobbery is still to be found, particularly among those people who think they *ought* to be exhibiting a deep knowledge of wine in front of their dinner guests and make a display of elaborate ritual whilst patently knowing no more about it than the man in the street. It is to be found, too, in the more exclusive hotels, in the exchanges between obsequious wine waiters and their *nouveau riche* customers.

At the other end of the scale, I think we are almost 'brainwashed' into choosing what can only be called 'plonk', at its worst, and 'acceptable', at its best, from our shops. Famous for our conservative natures and our mistrust of foreign-sounding names, we plump for the safe and familiar, offered at attractive prices.

All this is now coming to an end. More varieties of wine are in our shops arousing our curiosity, we are travelling abroad more than ever before, particularly to France in view of its proximity, and what country could possibly boast more variety of wines to be sampled than France? The aim of this book is to encourage you to branch out from your British reserve and go discovering for yourselves the wines of France growing in their native region and produced on the spot.

The advantages of doing so are multiple. You can choose to explore the products of absolutely any of France's wine regions, (and there are very few areas where wines are not produced), whilst at the same time enjoying the kind of holiday you prefer, whether it's soaking up the sun by the Mediterranean, or tramping over the hills in the Vosges. Every region will have some sort of wine to offer, from the most exclusive down to the most ordinary, everyday bottle. Some regions, such as the Loire, will offer widely differing types of wine, sparkling, rosé, white and red, each of these categories even sub-dividing into individual flavours and strengths, all to be found within easy reach of each other.

Apart from the advantage of variety and choice, there is that of price. Anything bought direct from the area of origin is bound to be much cheaper than the same product bought elsewhere after several middlemen and tax people have been involved, and nowhere, it seems, is this fact more manifest than in relation to wine. In

the area where it is produced, even your favourite 'special occasion' bottle becomes readily accessible, and the price of the more ordinary wines of the region allows you to sample from one district to another without needing to count the cost.

France's wine laws give a further advantage. Through their system of quality control they protect the vulnerable consumer, such as the visitor who has had little opportunity to experience wine. Every bottle declares on its label exactly what it is and where it has come from; once the visitor has understood the few basic facts to do with this control, he can feel safe in the knowledge that no-one will take advantage of his inexperience in the field.

A further obvious advantage of discovering your wines at source is that of being able to see first hand what processes are involved in the making of it before it reaches your table. It surely adds an extra dimension to the pleasure already received from enjoying a good glass of wine to have seen and understood how the vines are grown in different regions, how they are harvested and later vinified.

Finally, wines can be found which have never been heard of at home because they are simply not exported from France. You may not like all of them but until you try, they will surely remain a fascinating question mark. One of the aims of this book is to help you track down some of France's least known or least appreciated wine and let you decide for yourself whether you have found a gem or whether it is better left undiscovered.

Discovering wines at source in France may not sound like a highly original idea to those of you who have already driven through the country and sampled its wares – in fact it is pretty hard not to drive through certain areas without being pressed into some booth or '*caveau*' lining the streets of the most popular tourist spots. What is suggested throughout these pages is that there can be a lot more to sampling France's wine than simply stopping off in the great and famous areas thronged with other tourists doing exactly the same thing. Those vineyards which you are directed to by means of tourist brochures, roadside hoardings and guide books are the very ones to avoid! They are what one might commonly term 'geared up' for business: they have designed their tasting areas to seat as many as possible, their car parks will hold coaches, and their staff will be polite but are nevertheless just doing a job, and are possibly tired of seeing endless holiday-makers who appear to have no feeling for wine whatsoever.

Likewise, the advice will be to avoid buying your wine in the many shops which the main towns of the regions will sport; restaurants, hotels and wine co-operatives are also out. The reasoning behind this advice is as follows: when you taste and buy from any of these places, the service you are being given is not a personal one in the true sense of the word. The shop assistant has not played any part in growing the grapes which have gone into your wine and can only give you limited help in making your choice – the larger the shop the less help you will receive. Some shops will not even be able to let you taste before buying, thus putting you at a disadvantage immediately. In a restaurant or hotel you can certainly try the local wine, but when it comes to buying it by the bottle to take home, you will be paying far more than if it were purchased direct from the grower. The large wine co-operative is exactly what it sounds like and represents a 'pooling' of local growers' harvests, thus nearly always resulting in a blended wine made up of good, bad or indifferent produce, instead of being the product of one single vineyard, made by one man. Again, the service will not be personal and there will be no 'atmosphere' as a co-operative will probably be rather like a factory. Except in certain circumstances, when you might be unable to locate a grower, a visit is not recommended.

You may well ask where you *can* go to taste the local wine. There are only the grand châteaux left and they don't look as though they would welcome holiday-makers seeking to buy the odd bottle or two, even if they could afford it. This assumption is basically right, although there are a few notable exceptions which will be mentioned later.

Wine is one of the noblest cordials in nature.
JOHN WESLEY

The answer lies in the secret vineyards, tucked away and hidden from the well-worn tourist tracks. The secret vineyards are where the land has been in the same family's possession for generations, where the skills of growing vines and making wine have been passed on from father to son, where no main roads pass by and few tourists penetrate. These vineyards may not have distinguished themselves enough to be marked on a map and, admittedly, their wines may not measure up to those sold at the grander properties, but they will be a true product of that very spot, grown by the man you will meet, and he will be fiercely proud of them.

It is during your quest for such vineyards that you will see the real countryside at work, breathe its special atmosphere, and meet the people actually involved in all the hard work and frustrations, instead of those employed to put over an image. Surely this kind of exploration is much more worthwhile than the other easier option? First, locate the well-known area, which is most likely where everybody else is heading if it is the height of the season, then deliberately choose the most unlikely looking side road or cart track and begin your own personal search; it is always far more rewarding and always leads to the unexpected.

These vineyards should be your aim if you wish to imbibe the true atmosphere of French wine-making country but don't avoid altogether the many interesting aspects of the well-known areas. The Médoc district of Bordeaux, for instance, is highly endowed with châteaux in the most literal sense of the word – true castles, often complete with turrets and moats, many of them awe inspiring, and some surrounded by beautifully laid out parks. Other widely known regions have châteaux which are like stately mansions. (In France's wine country the word château actually means a wine estate.) These are all part of the French wine scene and naturally must be visited if you find yourselves in the area, so do visit these great places, such as Château

Lafite, even take a guided tour round their cellars to see how they operate, but, having taken your photographs and enjoyed the experience, then turn off the main road in pursuit of your personal vineyard to make your purchases and feel the local pulse of wine-making.

At this stage, having, it is hoped, encouraged readers to indulge their taste for wine and perhaps get just a little excited at the prospect of a journey of discovery off the beaten track, it is probably correct to anticipate one major query – how do we begin? It is a good question. When faced with practically the whole of France to choose from with perhaps only two or three weeks' holiday, and naturally wanting to have a thoroughly good time, as well as finding out lots about wine, how indeed does one begin, particularly if the country or language is unfamiliar?

To try and resolve this situation the book is divided into two parts: the first is designed to provide all the information needed to give the confidence and direction you might be seeking if wine-hunting is a new activity, and the second is designed to give explicit and detailed help, including maps, for exploring every wine region of France. It is good to understand something of the background to French wine-making, what is involved in the actual growing of the vines, how much depends on the weather at crucial times, what kind of work goes on during which seasons, and so forth. All these facts help to make travelling time more interesting and enable you to appreciate so much more the furrows on a grower's brow or the callouses on his wife's hands, apart from the delicious product in your glass. An insight will also be given into the actual wine-making process, so that when you are invited to look round a grower's establishment and he rattles on in rapid French explaining it all to you, you will at least be able to understand the gist of the work without needing to be a linguist. Some basic background knowledge, however little, will stand you in very good stead when it comes to a visit to a secret vineyard, for the farmer will sense that you are really interested and not just wanting to buy his cheap wine and dash off elsewhere.

The quality control system of France is also explained, which will enable you to read the labels of bottles on offer and feel confident that you have a fair idea of what you are buying as far as good value is concerned. Guidance will then be offered on actually planning a sortie and narrowing your field of exploration down to the district whose wines you would like to explore. This idea of planning might make the whole thing sound rather like a military exercise and exactly the opposite of what a relaxing holiday should be, but we have found from experience that aimless wandering about in a wine region hoping, Micawber-fashion, for something to turn up magically in the shape of an idyllically situated vineyard does not work. It leads to frustration, short tempers and an eventual turning in to a tourist trap in defeat.

Finally, advice is offered on the actual tasting procedure itself, which should be the culminating point of your foray into the back streets and hills. No two tastings are exactly alike, but there are certain ways of going about the pleasant task which help you to enjoy the event, and knowing a little bit about etiquette in advance will make you feel at ease. Your host, too, will be pleased to see that you are not about to make any awful gaffes and will enjoy helping you if he has time to spare; when this happens, even with limited linguistic ability, it can lead to some truly memorable moments and often results in permanent friendship.

The second part of the book is specifically for use when travelling and will divide into the main areas of France's wine production, each area having its own particular wine information and a map to show the best regions. 'Up and coming' regions for exploration will be mentioned so that the traveller can choose whether to do some real pioneering in the backwoods, or play safe and select a vineyard close to those which already have made a name for themselves. It will be pointed out in this section that certain areas of France, notably the vast area in the south known as the Midi, cannot really be said to have produced any 'noble' wines of any distinction, but this does not mean to say that you will not have fun discovering just what it is that makes these wines a product of their region.

It is hoped that the question 'How do we begin?' will now be receding into the background, to be replaced by 'When shall we go?'. The months to avoid in France, if you can, are July and August, the *vacances* or holiday period, when traffic will be heavy and hotels and campsites full. September and October would be an ideal time for seeing the harvest, whereas if you go in late May or June, the weather is pleasant and the crowds have not begun.

Two final pieces of advice could perhaps be added here without being out of place, the first concerning wine snobbery. Articles appear in magazines and books by highly qualified people whose business is wine and who undoubtedly know what they are talking about, even though the language they use often sounds rather flowery and sometimes positively *chemical*. When all is said and done however, the pleasure of wine is a highly personal and individual matter and whatever the wine buffs say about a wine, the only thing which concerns us is whether *we* like it or not. Therefore, by all means be aware of the recommendations of connoisseurs, for they will be well founded, but keep an open mind as you experience the various wines on your travels, and don't be put off something 'inferior' simply because you think you ought to be preferring something 'better'.

Lastly, as a matter of courtesy, if for no other reason, do try to have a few French phrases to hand even if they are quite simple. It is a commonly held belief throughout Europe that the British will not try to use a little of someone else's language and appear to take offence when no English is offered in return. Even if your limit is '*Dégustation s'il vous plaît?*' as in the case of my husband, it will go a long way toward *entente cordiale*.

WINE AND COUNTRY

When travelling through vine-growing countryside, either by car or on foot, it is a good idea to know something of the work that is going on in the fields; the journey takes on an added interest enabling you to relate the work to the final product you are seeking at your selected vineyard. Furthermore, some of the drama involved in wine-production will come alive for you. The *vigneron*'s life is fraught with crucial decisions to do with the timing of certain operations and he is at the mercy of the weather, as all farmers the world over; one can sense the tension in the atmosphere on certain cold, clear evenings, for instance, when talking to a *vigneron*. Will there be a frost? A frost in May could have a devastating effect on the farmer's next vintage, particularly if he has only the one small area of vines and they are at a vulnerable stage in their growth. It is not only the smaller growers who become anxious in May as the flower buds form. Having asked the proprietor of the prosperous Château de Barbe at Bourg, on the Gironde, about the weather one May, and his predictions for the year's vintage, his face took on a worried frown as he looked up at the sky and talked of the '*lune rousse*', or April moon, that the area was currently suffering from, causing cold weather and frost danger.

Let's take a look at exactly what is involved in the production of wine, from planting to bottling. First and foremost, the grower must have a thorough knowledge of his land and likely local weather patterns in order to match up the grape he chooses to grow there. More detailed information about grape varieties can be found in the regional section of the book and the reader may be surprised to see just how many different sorts there are. The choice does not always lie with the *vigneron* however, for in some districts the rigidly controlled French wine laws specify which grape varieties are permitted when sanctioning wines of high quality. In Burgundy, for instance, to qualify as a classed growth, the Pinot Noir has to be used for red wine and the Chardonnay for white.

When he has the choice, the farmer must first consider the kind of soil he has, whether it is very gravelly, whether there is a lot of chalk in it, and so on, and he has to judge the drainage ability of the land. The lie of the vineyard is also of great importance; ideally the sun should shine on the vines from morning till night. Is there any protection from the wind, or are frosts more likely to be a hazard here than anywhere else? 'Microclimate' is the technical word which denotes the particular attributes of a small parcel of land in relation to position, weather and soil conditions. The fact that a certain vineyard has a favourable microclimate could well make all the difference to the finished product. Even the neighbouring vineyard, though looking very similar to the other in the eyes of a casual passer-by, could be producing a different flavour or body in its wine, accountable only by the fact that its microclimate is quite different.

Secondly, the *vigneron* must decide whether he wants quality or quantity when choosing his grape variety. The Carignan grape grown in the south of France, for example, produces plenty of quantity but needs other grapes to be added at vinification time in order to make any quality of flavour apparent.

A third consideration is that the variety chosen must match up with the type of vine stocks the farmer uses, as most vines are now grafted onto American stocks since the devastation caused by phylloxera in the late nineteenth century. (see p.24)

The *vigneron's* methods of farming vines obviously have a great bearing on the finished product. The traveller through France's vineyards will notice that in some areas the vines are trained to grow low to the ground, in others they might grow rather like rose bushes, and elsewhere they could be trained along wires. There is good reasoning behind each of these methods, just as there is behind the method of pruning chosen. In order to achieve a high-quality wine which corresponds with the regulations of the French wine laws, severe pruning is observed to limit the crop to the required density, but in the south for instance, where quantity is more the order of the day for some, the *vigneron* can be more relaxed on this aspect of care.

There is a right time for spraying against rot or insects; weeding and drainage demand attention, shoots have to be painstakingly tied to wires – these and many other routine jobs are to be seen as you pass through. (I am addicted to the *smell* of a vineyard in late May or early June, I cannot describe it, but to me it is very French.)

Harvest time is obviously critical for the *vigneron*. The countdown to the day when he judges his grapes to be perfect for picking, from the moment he sees that they have ripened, must be at times nerve wracking, at best exciting for him. He knows that there will be a moment when the balance of sugar and acidity is just right, it is something he must *feel* rather than see, and when this moment arrives he must get the job done as quickly as possible, for much could depend on it. At the same time he has to keep a sharp eye open for weather changes, for a heavy rain just at the crucial period could turn a top quality vintage into a mediocre one, as the grapes would swell and the resulting juice, or must, would be literally watered down leading to a much less concentrated wine.

Let's imagine that most of us travel through France between the months of May and October and set out a work plan so that you can be aware of what is happening in a typical French vineyard during this period.

MAY

In May the leaves have sprouted and are still very tender for facing possible frosts. In northern areas where frost is a permanent nightmare, one method of avoiding the consequences is to set up a water-spraying device over the vines which results in the water being frozen and protecting the delicate plants. This is done particularly in the district of Chablis. The alternative method is to provide some kind of heating to warm the air and keep the frost at bay, but the difficulties involved here are obvious. In May the soil is ploughed up and weeds killed, also crop-spraying is very much in evidence, to counteract insects or rot. Spraying is often carried out by helicopter when there are extensive tracts of vineland to sweep over, thus making the expense worthwhile, but this does seem to take some of the time-honoured romance out of the work. Those Frenchmen who still prefer the use of horses and oxen to the tractor must surely feel the same? The painstaking work of removing unwanted suckers from the vinestock is carried out at this time, and in the latter part of the month, tiny flower buds form.

JUNE

These tiny buds develop into flowers. In Alsace an old *vigneron* told me that between the 16th and 21st June would be the critical time for him at Ammerschwihr, when the buds would burst and any wild weather would be nigh fatal. He predicted a poor vintage in view of the very cold weather they were having and looked altogether despondent as he was only a small grower and needed his income. It was then that I first realised how crucial the vagaries of the weather can be, and how impotent the *vigneron* is in the face of them. The rapidly growing shoots are selected during June and tied up to the wires, poor ones being cut off. Spraying takes place and the tiny grapes begin to appear.

JULY

Men with knapsack sprayers trudge up and down, or machinery is employed to spray the vines with a copper sulphate preparation against mildew, this process taking place with monotonous regularity, and its aroma will certainly be noticeable if you are passing by. Straggling shoots are cut back in order that no effort is wasted by the vine and maximum growing power goes into the important area, the grapes themselves. Weeding could also be going on during this growing period, for it is of course not only the vines that are flourishing.

AUGUST

The grapes will be 'on the turn', taking on the colour they are noted for, according to variety. The ripening process now begins whilst the endless spraying against disease continues, and weeding could still be necessary.

SEPTEMBER

Trimming goes on until the last moment before harvest, though all spraying must come to a halt a few weeks before the *vendange* begins. Picking could be either by machine or manual, though the human method is far more interesting to watch for the tourist, and is still the one most frequently used. Desperately steep slopes will rely on human power and the Sauternes district, too, needs people, as will be seen later, for its very specialised selective picking. The harvest generally begins during the third week of ripeness.

OCTOBER

The harvest will last about a fortnight, then when the indoor work begins the land is prepared for another season, beginning with putting back some of the goodness taken out, i.e. fertilising. Often the pressed-out grape skins can be seen in use for this purpose, fresh from the press.

The work we are unlikely to see takes place in winter when the vines are pruned back according to specification. Cuttings are carefully taken from superior plants and the tiny slips planted in sand in a nursery for a season. In March, life begins to stir and ploughing starts, both to aerate the soil and uncover the bottom of the stock, which would have been covered at the end of the year for protection against frost damage. The spot where the vine is grafted onto the stock is specially vulnerable during winter but needs releasing in spring ready for the growing period. Sometimes work around the stocks and between the plants where the plough cannot reach is done by hand-raking. Endless tidying-up jobs will take place, and by April the grower will be planting out the slips which have been a year in the nursery. He will occasionally have to replace old vines or damaged ones, which have outlived their usefulness. This period of usefulness however can be as long as fifty years in some fine areas, the best vines being known for their longevity. The cycle begins again. . . .

To return now to our original question of what is involved in producing the wine we love, we have seen what the grower has to do out in the vineyard through the seasons and cannot help but realise that he is very much at the mercy of the elements at certain crucial stages of cultivation. When it comes to the actual vinification or wine-making process, however, modern technology and science can play an enormous part and can even counteract and compensate for various adverse conditions. The science of wine-making, oenology, is complex and will be left to the experts to study, but it is nevertheless a fascinating field. We propose here to simply outline the basic wine-making procedure and point out the different techniques which are involved in producing the various major types of wine.

A guided tour of a winery in an organised group can greatly add to your knowledge of wine, although it must be admitted that for me, the beauty and mystery of the luscious liquid was completely ruined when I was first shown round one of these up-to-the-minute, shiny-cylindered factories with sparkling floors, spotless machinery and everything organised with mechanical precision. Naturally, I understood that the wine resulting from all this would be top quality, but somehow the romance was missing. Far more interesting to me is the small château, where the grapes are growing on the nearby land and the equipment for wine-making, though hygienic, has character and could be quite old. An opportunity to see round one of these châteaux should be seized with enthusiasm for they represent the history of wine rather than its technological advances.

Back then to the basic wine-making process and a brief look at the stages involved in the turning of the harvested grapes into wine. The sequence of events for red and white differs:

WHITE WINE

White or red grapes can be used to make white wine and are first of all crushed in an *égrappoir* which removes their stalks. They then travel to a horizontal press where they are broken up and pressed, coming out into a trough under the new name of 'must', the skins having been discarded. The juice is white in spite of red skins, because there has not been sufficient time for the skins to impart any of their colour. From the trough the must is pumped into a fermentation vat and then three options are available:

1. Dry wine
This results when the juice is fermented completely and all its sugar turns to alcohol.

2. Sweet wine
The juice is removed before fermentation is complete, thus leaving a certain controlled amount of sugar. The addition of either alcohol or sulphur then stops further fermentation. Fine filtration could be another method used.

3. Sparkling wine
The juice is removed before fermentation is complete and allowed to continue in the bottle.

RED WINE

Red grapes go through the crusher and straight into the fermentation vat, complete with skins. Colour is transferred to the liquid and tannin also is absorbed into it during fermentation of up to a fortnight, then the wine is allowed to run off into the barrels without being pressed. The remaining skins are pressed into an unpleasant-tasting, strong, dark liquid which eventually will be mixed to the vintner's specifications with the unpressed wine.

ROSÉ WINE

The grapes, complete with skins, follow the red wine process, but the juice is allowed to become only slightly coloured before it parts company with the skins and goes into a fermentation vat to finish up usually as a dry wine.

AGEING, RACKING AND BOTTLING

Once the wine is safely in barrels or vats and is ready to begin the ageing process, the next job is to make sure that oxidation does not spoil the quality of the wine, through air coming into contact with it. The barrels are constantly topped up so that there is no 'ullage', the word given to the space between the top of a cask and the wine level, and for this reason the cask is only loosely stoppered. A period of secondary fermentation follows, particularly in the case of red wines, but modern technology is capable of dealing with this – it can be stopped if desired.

'Racking' or syphoning off the wine from its first barrel into a fresh clean one to prevent any staleness takes place when a wine is going to be kept in the wood for some time, and clarifying might also become necessary to remove any remaining solid matter, this latter process being called 'fining'.

Bottling time means yet another important decision for the wine-maker as different styles of wine ideally demand a different length of time before being bottled.

The *primeur*-style wines, those designed to be drunk almost immediately, are usually only given a few weeks before they are bottled and, of course, we read every year of the mad race to be there at the right time in order to fetch home the first bottle of Beaujolais, Beaujolais *nouveau*, hot off the press, as it were. At the other end of the scale comes the unusual wine peculiar to the Jura region which lies in the barrel for a minimum of six whole years before it is bottled, the vintner allowing a strange film to settle on top of the wine which is otherwise open to the elements in his cellar. No topping up is necessary in this case, the wine seals itself. In the relevant section of the book we can tell you just how to locate the Jura's famous *vin jaune*. Even after a lengthy time in the cask, many of the finer wines need several years in the bottle as well, before they are ready to be drunk, notably the great Bordeaux, Burgundies and sweet wines.

The subject of bottling should not be left without a mention of the cork. Yes, even such a mundane-sounding thing as a cork is important to the well-being of a great wine, though it must be admitted that the more ordinary the wine is and the more short-lived, the less important does the matter of the cork become. Those wines which require long keeping also require a long cork of excellent quality; a crumbly cork of poor quality which might let in air and undesirable foreign bodies could ruin in a moment something which has taken years of hard labour and much skill to achieve.

Some of the cork, incidentally, can be found in an area of France which is not wine-producing, namely the strange district called the Landes bordering the south-west coast, and it is also grown in the far south. The cork is the very thick bark of an evergreen oak variety, *quercus suber*, which can be carefully removed without killing the tree. Its advantage over other possible material for stopping up the bottles is that it gives no taste to the wine, unlike plastic or rubber for instance, and it shuts out the air so that the wine cannot oxidise yet still allows it to develop. A major advantage is that it is cheap although it is a matter of speculation how long this can remain so. The minimum standard length for a cork is 4.5cm (1¾in) and it most likely comes from bark with eight years' growth behind it. Slower-grown bark is used for the superb, expensive wines, having probably grown for twice as long as the common variety.

The final stage in the bottling process is of course the labelling, the French word for the label being *étiquette*, and in the following chapter you can discover how to read the information it gives.

The growing and wine-making processes have now been covered as far as basic rules go, but as ever there are always a few exceptions, so under the broad title of background knowledge a couple of these are described. Chaptalisation pertains to the alchohol in a wine, and *pourriture noble* to a specific method of harvesting the grapes.

CHAPTALISATION

This is a process whereby extra sugar is added to the unfermented juice, when a grower realises from testing a small amount of must that it is not going to produce a wine with the amount of alcohol in it which he wishes. He is legally allowed to add this sugar in most regions, and the wine laws of France, which will be discussed in the following chapter, keep an eagle eye on what he is doing. He must comply strictly with the regulations and is even obliged to give the authorities advance notice before he goes ahead. Particularly in the north this procedure may become necessary, if the natural sugar in the must is not going to be sufficient to make a well-balanced or long-keeping wine. The subject of chaptalisation with the underlying implication that the natural wine is being somehow interfered with is often a thorny one, but all evidence points to the fact that it is truly beneficial when skilfully done.

POURRITURE NOBLE

This means 'noble rot' in English and is not nearly so nasty as it sounds – in fact it is music in the ears of a grower who specialises in making long-living sweet white wines. During the summer months endless spraying goes on right up to the last few weeks before the harvest, or *vendange*, the object being to prevent *botrytis*, a mildew infection. However, there is one kind of wine which strangely thrives on this very same organism, *botrytis cinerea*, given the right conditions of weather at the right time of year. In France this wine is made chiefly in the Sauternes district and in the Vouvray area of the Loire. The conditions needed to turn this potentially damaging mildew into something beneficial are cool nights, giving way to misty autumnal mornings and warm, dry days. The rot does not follow the pattern it might do in wet weather after the spraying has had to stop, but instead penetrates the skin of the grapes so slowly that they begin to wither and dry up, resulting in a corresponding concentration of sugar and flavour in the juice and yielding only a very small amount of sweet, dessert wine.

The snag to all this is that, as mentioned previously, the harvest is a very special one, when people are needed to go through the vineyard selecting only a few bunches at a time when they are at their 'nobly rottenest' and probably have to do this on half a dozen separate occasions in order to catch the grapes when they are exactly right. The small grower in such areas is immediately presented with a problem, for he cannot afford to pick in this manner; he must make a brave decision and harvest it all at once. Imagine the plight of a grower who waits and waits, hoping for the exact conditions to arise, and then along comes the bad weather – he could risk having no vintage at all.

PHYLLOXERA

Phylloxera is a subject which features regularly in any discussion of the history of the vine, for it is the name of a disease brought to Europe from America in the second half of the nineteenth century, which wreaked havoc wherever it spread. In France the period of devastation was the 1870s and 1880s when most vineyards were all but destroyed and had to be painstakingly rebuilt.

The cause of the destruction was found to be a louse of American origin which attacked the roots of the vinestock, and was introduced to Europe on vines sent over from the United States. The idea of grafting native vines onto American stocks which are resistant to the louse was put into practice and found to work, but it meant that many years of production were lost, some vineyards which already had difficulties in viticulture couldn't cope and went into decline, and the long-life factor of the vine was affected. The new vines do not live as long as formerly, giving rise to the discussion as to whether the quality of the wines produced pre-phylloxera was higher than that of today, since the older the vine the better the quality of its grapes in general.

GETTING TO KNOW THE COUNTRY

The object so far of this chapter has been to give the traveller a basic background knowledge of vine growing and wine-making, without becoming too technical or clinical, in order to impart a deeper understanding of what will be seen in France's wine regions. This is important for two reasons, firstly because everything to do with wine and its production can then take on a new interest and add an extra dimension to a holiday, and secondly because it helps bring the traveller into closer contact with the people of France.

It follows that if you as the visitor to the country are able to show a real interest in what you are seeing and can communicate this interest to the people you are meeting, whether they are the growers themselves or just people in shops, cafés or campsites, you will automatically come that much closer to knowing the character of the people you are among. They will all be closely connected with wine if they live in the regions you are exploring, in fact it will be a part of their way of life, and as is the way with all enthusiasts, they will be happy to talk about it.

This is not to say, of course, that you are expected to have learned discussions on wine and weather wherever you go, even if you are a proficient French speaker, that would be boring, but it leads to other interesting experiences, it forms an introduction, as it were, to the local people. My husband, on one famous occasion, just happened to point to the bottle of local wine we were enjoying with our picnic and made appreciative, universally understood noises as the farmer whose field we were in passed by, and lo and behold we were invited into the ancient farmhouse kitchen that evening to taste *his* bottle and meet his family. Today we are still in touch, having made a friendship through simply sharing a common interest, wine, and showing our appreciation of the regional variety. The wine talk led to an interesting evening exchanging ideas and seeing how a farmer's family lived, and to his showing us round the nearby special cattle market the following day. He also told us where to go to discover a slightly different local wine, which we would otherwise never have found.

For the person who wants more out of his holiday than the well-worn tourist routes and hotels have to offer, it is essential to have a knowledge of where all the smaller 'local' places are likely to be, and what they in contrast have to offer. The best thing to do is to consult one of the up-to-date books giving details of gîtes and farmhouses in France. Some will be more appropriate than others, according to how deeply you want to immerse yourselves in a local environment, and choosing somewhere can be an exciting part of planning your wine trip. Ideally, the places to choose will be those which let you live *en famille* with your French host and hostess, whether just for overnight stays or for a longer period. *Chambre d' hôte* is the sign to look out for when you are ready to be put up for the night – the equivalent of our 'bed and breakfast'. What better or more pleasurable way could there be of getting the feel of French regional country life than sitting down to a typical breakfast of that area with the family, being able to chat about their work, their problems, their pastimes and in turn telling them about our ways?

Sampling the local food can be every bit as interesting as sampling the wines since food is another intrinsic part of the local heritage. In the regional chapters following, the reader will find a few remarks about what specialities are to be found in each area. In general we tend to think in terms of trying these regional foods in restaurants. A well-chosen restaurant will, of course, prepare the local speciality, but how much more interesting it would be to sample it in a farmhouse kitchen, see the big pots steaming, see how the housewife prepares her food, in contrast perhaps to some of our methods. In the country, everyone stops everything for two hours around midday to have the main meal, *déjeuner* – men returning home, school children too. Conversation is noisy in big families, and the meal is an event to be lingered over, not to be done with as quickly as possible, as so often in our bustling cities at home.

The main course of *déjeuner* is always preceded by some kind of a *hors d'oeuvre*, however simple, designed to look nice and whet the appetite for the major part of the meal. The ubiquitous French bread is present, of course, throughout the whole of the meal and is eaten plain, without butter. A green salad usually follows the main course to clean the palate, and a French countrywoman would probably be aghast to see that our own green salad nearly always means lettuce. She makes use of a grand selection of green leaves and will toss them in a delicate dressing at the last possible moment before serving. Cheese, fruits or nuts are likely to follow and a cup of black coffee. Incidentally, if there is a dessert, it always comes after the cheese, not before, as in Britain. The reason is connected with wine: it enables the guests to finish their main course wine with the savoury cheese course instead of probably leaving it when it doesn't go with the sweet things which follow. If another wine is offered, it can then come out with the dessert and be lingered over.

Wine will always be present during the meal as it is a fact of everyday life. If you find yourself staying in a farmhouse or private guesthouse deep in wine country, this must surely be the best way of tasting what the locals drink, even though it may not be the kind of bottle you would choose to buy and take home. Common sense tells us that it will not be the best wine of the area, but it will be what the French call *typé* of the region. If you find they are not drinking local wine at all, there must be a very good reason, which you can soon ascertain for yourself! I will go on to explain why I advise against buying poorer quality local wines to take home later in the book, but in the meantime I will assume that the traveller in wine country will be interested in trying wines at all levels, from the best he can afford to the simplest family wine.

A little has been written about meeting the country people of the region and understanding something of their way of life, which might to some readers appear as a digression from our main theme of wine, but this can be disputed. 'No man is an island' is an often quoted phrase but the British live on an island and do tend to be very insular in outlook. France is just across the Channel and is riddled with tiny, unexplored routes in many little-visited areas, many of them yielding up secret vineyards for the seeking. Why must we stick doggedly to the seaside resorts and Paris, where we feel relatively safe in the knowledge that there are plenty of other English-speaking people, and anyway we won't need to say much in French because they're all used to us by now?

It is hoped this chapter will have inspired you to want to go further inland than before, to really get to know something of rural France in its everyday garb, to meet its people on friendly terms, using smiles and sign language if nothing else is available, as well as to achieve your aim of feeling that you now know enough about wine to get the maximum enjoyment out of your visit.

Meet the people actually involved in all the hard work and frustrations, instead of those employed to put over an image

UNDERSTANDING LABELS

Since this book is written primarily to help non connoisseurs to find their way about the grand variety of French wines which they are likely to encounter on their travels, we propose in this section to describe the French methods of labelling. These methods when properly understood tell the purchasers all they need to know in order to feel reasonably confident that they are spending their money wisely and getting what they want in return.

France is streets ahead of most other wine-producing countries in its well-established wine laws and, although there are the inevitable loopholes to be found, as with all laws if someone is determined or unscrupulous enough to look for them, they have resulted in being happily advantageous to both grower and consumer alike. In brief, the French have a quality control system which transfers itself in writing as a kind of guarantee on the bottle label for everyone to see. The system is basically simple, but for the benefit of those who have not yet come across it, it is proposed now to draw an analogy to make it come alive.

The laws are known as *Appellation d'Origine Contrôlée*, meaning controlled name of origin, and exist to regulate certain factors involved in the production of wine in a particular area. It is therefore important first of all to understand what this 'name of origin' refers to. The analogy I am going to use is that of a London address. Below is a typical London address and next to it, a Bordeaux one:

Bob Smith,   Monsieur X,
2 Brickworks Row,   Château Coutet,
Bow,   Barsac,
E.3.,   Sauternes,
London.   Bordeaux.

We shall compare this address in London with the wine region of Bordeaux and go on to show how just as the London address narrows itself down to one particular house, so the wine region narrows itself down to one particular château.

Londoners are a different kind of people from the rest of England we feel, just as Bordeaux wine is in general a different kind of wine from any of the others in France,

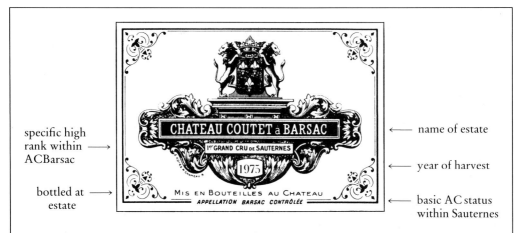

specific high
rank within
ACBarsac

bottled at
estate

← name of estate

← year of harvest

← basic AC status
within Sauternes

so the two words immediately make us focus on the general qualities which go into their make-up. The district of E.3. in London makes us think of Eastenders, a people known for their happy-go-lucky natures, amongst other things. The district of Sauternes in Bordeaux is just one of the several distinct areas within the Bordeaux wine region and makes us think of the very sweet white wine it specialises in. Bow is a district within E.3., its distinguishing feature being perhaps its street markets, whereas Barsac is a small district within Sauternes having certain distinguishing features in its Sauternes-style wine which mark it as being different from the other communes nearby. At 2 Brickworks Row lives Bob Smith, who is the man who works the jellied eel stall on his local market, whereas at Château Coutet there lives a wine grower who produces a very special wine, distinguishing itself by its high quality.

The progression of individuality is what we are hoping to point out here, for this is how the body applying the *Appellation Contrôlée* law works. Wine which is made within the broad Bordeaux region does not have to meet many requirements to gain the words *Appellation Bordeaux Contrôlée* on its label, but the more specific the place name becomes, the harder it is to qualify for an appellation. Château Coutet wine has to pass rigorous tests in order to gain the award of its own *Premier Grand Cru* status – it is an individual among the general, just as Bob Smith is a specialist trader among his fellow traders.

The smaller the area of wine within its 'parent' region and the more specific the name or appellation awarded it, the higher is the indication of relative quality to the consumer, and the higher will be the price required by the grower, hence the mutual benefit mentioned above. The grower will normally choose to put on his label the most specific appellation he has qualified for, and fraud inspectors exist to make sure that the laws are not abused.

It is interesting to have some idea of the restrictions placed upon growers who aspire to ever higher standards of quality, as they relate well to what was discussed in the previous chapter. As has been noted already, the area of production for each place

the property →  ← father and son, growers, since 1836

Viticulteurs de Père en Fils depuis 1836

Cheverny

APPELLATION D'ORIGINE VIN DÉLIMITÉ DE QUALITÉ SUPÉRIEURE

← name of appellation area

← VDQS status

DJ 801

Mis en bouteille   *à la propriété par*

← bottled at the property

75 cl   GAEC GIVIERGE PÈRE & FILS viticulteurs   PRODUCE OF FRANCE

41700 COUR CHEVERNY

TÉL. 54 79 98 17   FILIBER NUITS - Reprod. inter...

local address → of growers

name or appellation has to be strictly defined, its boundaries set and observed. Secondly, grape varieties to be used are specified, for example the Pinot Noir is to be used in the Côte d'Or and Chalon areas of the Burgundy region. The choice of grape is always made with reference to what has proved best in the past for the traditional methods of particular areas. A minimum alcohol content must also be reached before a wine qualifies for appellation, this figure being governed by pruning methods basically. The amount of wine produced per hectare from that area is governed too, and strict control is also kept on growing and wine-making practices. Apart from all these controls most *Appellation Contrôlée* wines are tasted by a panel of experts before acquiring status.

These laws reached their present form in 1936, but in 1949 there followed the creation of a 'second class' system, known as *Vins Délimités de Qualité Supérieure* (VDQS), or delimited wines of superior quality. Regulations governing the production of these lesser wines are similar to those of AC rank, but not nearly so strict, yet the term 'lesser' must not be used in a derogatory sense by any means. It ought to be explained here that these wines in the first classification group represent France's finest, but in view of the fact that the system encourages better methods of growing and vinification, growers are aspiring all the time, particularly with the aid of recent technological advances, to improve their quality. As a result of this the VDQS found on a label represents a very good wine, far superior to the tremendous amount of *vin ordinaire* produced in France in general.

Just to prove how the system works, in 1973 a third classification was introduced, that of *Vin de Pays*, or wine of the country, meaning local wine. These wines represent the better wines emerging from the *vin ordinaire* category, which could be from anywhere at all in France. *Vin de Pays* is the one to be watched with interest, for it has potential for the future, although the wine connoisseur would most likely not take any notice of it.

the estate ↓

a name for his own blend →

← bottled at the domaine

← grape variety used for this wine

← name of estate

Vin de Pays → status proprietor/grower's name and → local address

← French table wine

CHARDONNAY
Domaine de Fourn
Vin de Pays de l'Aude
Vin de Table Français
75 cl
ROBERT GFA - Propriétaire récoltant à Pieusse
Aude France

This, then, is how France divides her wines into quality-based groups and the bottle label witnesses to the fact. You can be sure that what the label tells you is true, so a little must now be said about reading the label itself. Since wine-lovers are encouraged to seek out regional wine with a 'home-grown' flavour to it, i.e. a taste which you could say was typical of that particular area, the words on the label relevant to this subject will be picked out first. These terms indicate that the wine is not a standardised blend made up of several vintages from a widely assorted area:

Mis en bouteilles au château *au domaine* *à la propriété*	Denotes that the wine was bottled at the property where it was made.
Propriétaire/viticulteur */récoltant*	Owner/grower, usually followed by his name and address in that area.

Words denoting standard of wine:

Appellation Contrôlée VDQS *Vin de Pays*	The place name will follow one of these to denote origin of wine.

The above are the basic facts on the label which enable you to know that your wine is of a certain standard, as described, and is homegrown.

When a wine is not home produced and bottled on the estate where grown, it could be:

1   Exported by a firm of shippers and bottled by the importer.
2   Purchased by a wine dealer and matured by him until ready for sale.

3 Made and bottled in a wine co-operative, using the produce of many local growers all together.

   In the first case, the label will state clearly the name of the shippers or importers, leaving you in no doubt. The second case warrants an explanation of the term *négociant/éleveur* which will appear on the label.

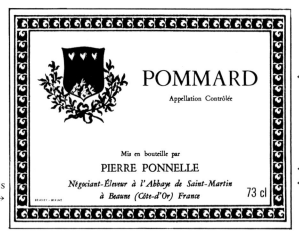

AC of commune where harvest comes from

bottled by Pierre Ponnelle

négociant status of the above

négociant's address (note it is not the same as area harvested)

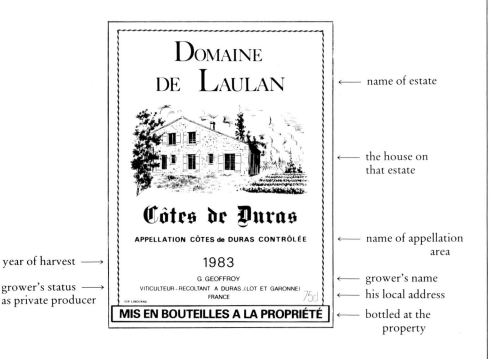

name of estate

the house on that estate

name of appellation area

grower's name

his local address

bottled at the property

year of harvest

grower's status as private producer

NÉGOCIANT/ÉLEVEUR

Négociant is the French word for the dealer or businessman whose job is to purchase wine directly from the growers and take over the rest of its 'education', (hence the word *éleveur*, one who 'brings on' a product), until he bottles it and markets it, under his name plus the name of origin. This middleman tends to be useful when the grower, particularly one who owns only a very small area of a large estate, such as those growers typical of Burgundy, has not the facilities or sufficient technical know-how to make the best of the vinification process.

Since the advice is to seek out the small but reliable grower/proprietor, the produce of the *négociant* would not be recommended; it could be said that his wine must lose something of the individuality the small grower's wine displays and would naturally be more expensive, having involved a third party.

CO-OPERATIVES OR UNIONS VITICOLES

These establishments fulfil a much needed function for the small growers who simply cannot afford to buy and maintain the equipment required for good vinification. They sell their vintage, along with that of their neighbours in the region, to the local wine union which is capable of taking in the whole area's produce, each grower having his contribution assessed as it is brought in for quality and quantity and receiving a docket to be produced later when the wine has been vinified and marketed. The advantages to the grower are great, since not only does he have an immediate sale for his produce, but he is also saved the trouble of marketing, advertising, etc. He becomes a share-holder literally, and receives a share in the company's profits. The co-operative also receives the poorer quality material from

co-operative cellars and address →

→ typical countryside

→ name of appellation area

→ Basque country and proud of it!

→ bottled at the property

→ AC status

IROULEGUY

CAVE COOPÉRATIVE
S⁺-ÉTIENNE DE BAIGORRY
(PYRÉNÉES-ATLANTIQUES)
FRANCE

PAYS BASQUE

MIS EN BOUTEILLES A LA PROPRIETE

APPELLATION IROULÉGUY CONTROLÉE   75cl

the better-known growers, who have no wish to lower their name by selling an inferior label next to their more prestigious one.

It is obvious, therefore, that the wine produced in this way will be a blend of local produce, not the produce of one vineyard, even though it could be expertly made. It happens occasionally that in some areas, particularly in the South of France, it is impossible to buy a bottle of the local wine from a private producer, as it all goes to the co-operative, but apart from such cases, these places should be avoided for purchasing. Their name will be clearly visible on the label.

Sometimes growers like to add their own touch to a label which is designed to tell the buyer a little more about the wine. Below are a few extras occasionally seen on labels:

Médaille d'Or, d'Argent, de Bronze, etc.	Prizes won for that wine
The *cépage*, e.g. Sauvignon	Grape variety used
Cuvée plus name, or *Cuvée Réservée*	Special 'brew'
Name of one of their vineyards	Indicates individuality

In the next chapter advice will be given on how to locate those vineyards which have not made a name for themselves but which have interesting wines on offer, yet it has to be admitted that for some, it is difficult to pass through a famous region without acquiring at least a bottle or two of something with a reputation, to take home for those very special occasions we all have in mind. Further assistance with label reading now becomes necessary since the finer wines often have classifications of their own which can at first appear confusing.

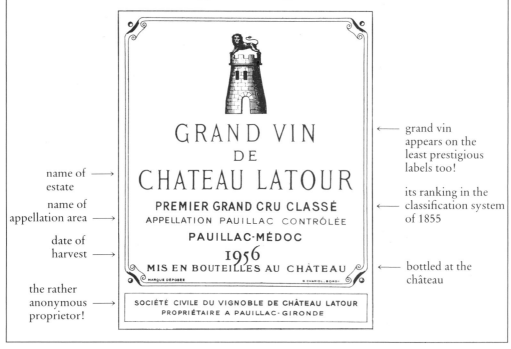

name of estate →

name of appellation area →

date of harvest →

the rather anonymous proprietor! →

← grand vin appears on the least prestigious labels too!

← its ranking in the classification system of 1855

← bottled at the château

Médoc wines, in particular, seem to have complicated labels when they reach a certain standard. In 1855, the top growths (or *crus*) were organised into a grand system of classification which has remained very much the same even to this day with a few exceptions, attracting much criticism. Below we give the gist of this system:

1 *Grand Cru Classé* or *Cru Classé*	This subdivides into five numbered *crus*, *premier*, *deuxième*, etc. but only *premier* is the one commonly written on the label.
2 *Cru Bourgeois*	Subdivides into several categories of pecking order, using the words *grand*, *exceptionnel* and *supérieur*.

After the *Crus Bourgeois* come the six *commune* appellations to be found in the Bordeaux chapter (p.84).

Burgundy is the other area you might be tempted to spend in, and its labelling system differs from that of Bordeaux because of the small parcels into which its vineyards are broken up (p.99). Below is the gist of this system:

1 The name of the parish or *commune* often features largest on the label.
2 The name of the individual *climat* comes next, *climat* being literally one 'field' of the larger vineyard.

3 *Grand Cru*	Top growth
4 *Premier Cru*	Next in high quality

Those are the two types of label you are likely to be gazing at in awe if you do indeed decide to treat yourself to an expensive souvenir, plus perhaps those of Champagne. Since Champagne is an entirely different type of wine from that which has so far been discussed, its label language will appear in the section devoted to Champagne itself in the regional chapters. The Alsace label too has its own language

name of → appellation area

bottled by → the *négociant*

the commune name ←

← the *climat* or individual vineyard

← name of *négociant*

← status of Louis Latour and his address (note it is not Aloxe-Corton)

and though Alsace would not perhaps be classified as one of the above-mentioned 'greats', its label is described likewise in the regional section.

There are a few words to be found on labels which do appear to be misleading, though whether this is a deliberate intention on the part of the bottler, or just a part of sales technique, is a matter for speculation.

Haut	Normally denotes something superior in quality, but means nothing at all on a label except as part of the appellation Haut-Médoc where it is used to distinguish it from Bas-Médoc, further north.
Grand Vin	Great wine. It most likely is too, but it has no legal right over those which do not use the description.
Mise dans nos caves	Literally 'bottled in our cellars', which to the amateur label-reader might be a misleading statement, for it doesn't tell us by whom. If by the proprietor/grower it should say so, but otherwise the cellars could be anywhere, even in the importing country where the *négociant* or shipper does his bottling.

BEWARE OF FALSE CHÂTEAUX!

The word château simply means a wine-making property or estate. We naturally tend to envisage turrets, moats, drawbridges and the like, and attach an aura of grandeur to the word. Be prepared to be disappointed, therefore, when on reading château on a label you decide to track it down and see it for yourselves, for the home of the grower is most likely little more imposing than your own.

Beware, too, of thinking that the presence of the château's name and most likely its pretty picture, have anything to do with the quality of the wine. Remember that the name coupled with *Appellation Contrôlée* is your guide to quality or rank.

The three-tier system devised by France's wine law makers is proving highly successful for it has the effect of a promotion ladder, whereby growers with ambition and talent can be rewarded for their efforts with a step up the ladder on to the next rung. The science of oenology has brought about many changes for the better, particularly among the growers of poorer-quality wines. They are now replacing some of their vines with new varieties, and learning how to mix and match certain types to produce the best that can be said to be typical of that region. Their farming methods are being improved all the time and the inspectors who fan out in every direction to report on progress now take an interest in areas which in the past would not have even been worth a visit.

Each year sees the creation of new VDQS areas out of the former *Vin de Pays* class and a number of VDQS wines have proved their worth and climbed a rung to AC class. It is an ongoing event, unlikely to turn back now that it has gained momentum, especially as the wine-drinking fraternity is becoming more selective. The incentive to carry on improving is undoubtedly the fact that better wines mean better prices can be obtained for them, which in turn means that better equipment can be bought and the whole process gathers impetus.

About one third of all France's wine now falls into the *Appellation Contrôlée* class, this figure having risen rapidly during the last decade. It proves that the system can only lead to more wine of higher quality becoming available to all of us if we only care to seek it out. If we bear in mind the one or two points about misleading words, the basic three-tier system is not too difficult for anyone to follow, providing he does not get snarled up in what admittedly can become tricky, choosing one of the more exclusive wines of Bordeaux and Burgundy. As amateur consumers, we can feel protected by the knowledge that the authorities are keen on their work and have their watch dogs posted around the country. If we are new to the whole thing we have at least the comfort of knowing that if we take the trouble to study the labels, we will be able to some extent to sort out the sheep from the goats and make our choice accordingly.

CONFRÉRIES VINEUSES – WINE LODGES

These lodges or societies all over France began meeting in the Middle Ages to promote mutual brotherly aid, but gradually an interest in the quality of wine crept in. The Alsace *confrérie* is the oldest known, dating from the fourteenth century, but the most successful is probably the *Chevaliers du Tastevin* of Burgundy, and by success we mean commercial progress, for apart from thoroughly enjoying themselves at their traditional banquets in their ceremonial robes, they are very active in the promotion of their local wine. The St-Émilion *Jurade* is unusual in that its members still play an important part in the control of the quality of wine, (see p.96) but all of the *confréries* provide colourful folklore for their local festivals and entertainments.

IN SEARCH OF THE SECRET

The first questions you will probably ask yourself after deciding to turn your holiday, in part at least, into a wine-hunting event, are which wine, and where? One cannot help but notice from even a cursory flick through the regional chapters which follow, that there is an awful lot to choose from, more perhaps than you ever realised before you began to take wine more 'seriously'.

There are two main factors to take into consideration first, depending on how large a feature of your holiday wine tracking is likely to be. If you have decided you want to find out much more about the types of wine you are already familiar with, that is if you want to track down the genuine article and compare it with its imported version tried at home, all you need do is turn to the chapter dealing specifically with that kind of wine and let your planning begin there. If, however, the wine bibbing is to be a secondary part of your holiday, as for example when travelling with your family and pursuing other interests to keep everyone happy, then it's best to keep an open mind and when you find yourself in a 'viny' area, simply consult the chapters to see what is on offer there. Each chapter will tell you a little about what else there is to see and do, which might help in your choice, though to get a fuller picture of the area's opportunities, it's a good idea to pick up leaflets at local tourist information centres.

There will usually be several options open once you have arrived in the heart of a wine region, but the first thing to do is consult the map of the region to discover exactly where its heart is. There is no point in looking for a wine-tasting opportunity the moment you pass the first large hoarding or district name board which announces wine country, for in general, the closer you are to the tried and tested 'best' areas, the more chance there will be of finding a really good wine, typical of the region.

These 'best' areas are obviously very special in some way, so it is advisable to locate them, and have a walk around to see if you can spot anything which might make them stand out from the surrounding vineyards. What you have learnt from the chapter 'Wine and Country' regarding slopes, sun, methods of training, soil, and so on, can be put to good use during this exploratory time – try and see for yourselves what it might be that all these better vineyards share. Many of the good areas have anticipated the interest of the traveller and conveniently marked out a *route du vin*, or *route des grands crus*, as in the Médoc of Bordeaux, which saves you all the trouble of finding your own way about unfamiliar country. All you need to do is follow the signs, which in most places will be a bunch of grapes on a small notice; the whole family can have fun following these! The route will take you meandering through the heart of the best area, past all the famous châteaux, if indeed it is château country, and often leads you up into hills and slopes away from the villages below until you can see the whole district spread out from your vantage point.

Frequently, too, you can come across a *sentier*, or path, which takes you on a walk through the middle of the vineyard, literally along the terraces, past the little huts scattered about containing tools and other equipment. Here you can imagine for yourself the hard work, particularly when the land slopes steeply, you can feel the heat thrown up by a stony soil, you can smell the vines and see what stage they have reached; in other words, you begin to get a feel for all that goes into your good glass of wine.

Many of these footpath tours have plaques positioned along the route which tell the visitor what can be seen there, or simply give information in general about the grape varieties being used, the methods of growing, the seasonal work, and so on. These notices invariably consist of self-explanatory diagrams accompanied by just a few simple words of text, so that they are easily understood. They are useful in that they bring alive the information you might have taken in from reading before coming along to see for yourself.

> *And Noah he often said to his wife when he sat down to dine,*
> *'I don't care where the water goes, if it doesn't get into the wine.'*
>
> CHESTERTON

Having found the heart of the region, and maybe explored a little, you will have discovered what obvious tasting opportunities are available to you. Sometimes the choice may be bewildering, as for instance when you find yourself in the main tourist town of a popular area. The best thing to do under these circumstances is to sit down and take stock in a café, preferably the pavement or terrace type, with a glass of whatever is local at your elbow. The glass of 'local' will give you some idea of the regional wine, and the sit down gives you the chance to watch the world go by and absorb the atmosphere of the place whilst you make your choices. The co-operative is out of the question because you have seen that there are other opportunities here. The shop specialising in wines perhaps looks rather daunting – there are too many different looking types and labels; the assistant would be hovering over you, waiting for your request, and all the other customers look more knowledgeable than you. Apart from those reasons, it has already been said in the introductory pages that shops are out – no atmosphere, no personal interest or guidance with choice, no time to spare for talking to you, and above all, high prices. A supermarket would be 'safe', you could take your time reading the labels and find a local wine easily enough you might think. Yes, but the local wine you found would most likely only be the general run-of-the-mill one, undistinguished, and probably bought in bulk and specially bottled for the chain stores to sell under their brand name.

What is the answer? Either head for the nearest wine *village* or make for the surrounding area of vineyards nearest to the famous plots or châteaux. Our own first tour of the Bordeaux châteaux will serve as an illustration. We knew that any decent wine from the region north of Bordeaux was going to be fairly pricey, in comparison to some of the more nondescript wines of the south of France for instance, because poor quality is simply not produced where all the conditions are right for fine wine. There would be no point in just buying a 'Bordeaux red'. On the other hand we knew we could not afford to buy anything in the £30 to £40 per bottle bracket, such as is to be found at Château Lafite, for example. What we did was to locate the *route des grands crus* out of Bordeaux and follow its course through the famous Haut-Médoc area, taking in as we did so the seemingly endless châteaux, many of them clearly visible from the road, others hidden away, but leaving signposts to denote how one could find them. World famous names leapt out at us, Château Lafite, Mouton Rothschild, Latour – these were the ones whose produce had been consumed by the rich and privileged for years, and made auction news headlines at home in England. We drove up to Château Lafite and took photographs, even ventured into the reception area and witnessed a tourist spending a casual fortune on three bottles. It wasn't for us, the atmosphere was decidedly 'snooty' to say the least, but it was interesting none-the-less and gave us something to think about as we went off in pursuit of our own place, which turned out to be Château Moulin de la Rose in a St-Julien back street. We couldn't pretend that this was one of our most fascinating secret vineyards, in fact we did not even try to locate the vineyard itself, but we certainly have a few bottles of the '81 vintage which promises to be beautiful in a few years' time and which we are reserving for special occasions. The fact that it was located so close to Château Lafite caused us to stop there as there was obviously something very special about the conditions prevailing in those few acres.

We must pause here to reflect on personal taste and quality of wine. The wine at Château Lafite which we witnessed being purchased was indeed almost £40, we checked it on the price list, and it was their most 'ordinary' one. Our bottles were £4 each, and possibly worlds apart in quality, but the fact that we are not connoisseurs nor interested in paying extra for the prestige of a 'name' on the bottle meant that we were well satisfied with our purchase. How many general readers and wine lovers could really appreciate the difference in quality between our 'reasonable' bottle and the Lafite? It is not the intention here to insult anyone with a well-tutored palate, but merely to point out that most of us have not had, nor are likely to have, the opportunity to tutor that palate sufficiently to warrant paying for the finest of fine wines. The fact that the appellation was St-Julien and the wine was bottled at his château by the proprietor whose address was local, was all the guarantee we needed to know that we had bought good wine, typical of its area.

A further good reason for leaving the major tourist wine towns alone as far as purchasing goes is that you will get a far more accurate picture of everyday life in wine country by walking round the tiny villages and hamlets than by looking at windows full of souvenirs and tourist trash. These latter tend to be the same the world over. Isn't it far more interesting to see the old men gathering under the lime trees for their daily game of *boules*, berets on heads, faces often wizened as old apples, after a lifetime spent out in the vineyards in every weather, toiling up and down on foot before mechanisation took over? After a day's exploring when we recap in an evening over a bottle of something good, it always seems to be the little vignette of unchanged, unhurried local life which has stayed in our memories most – perhaps a glimpse of a nut brown, wrinkled old face, protected by a loosely-flapping head-covering against the sun, as granny contributed her effort to the family hay-making by dragging her old wooden rake slowly over the patch nearest to home. Or maybe it was the shepherd we saw deep in the Rhône area, black cape hung round his stooping figure, looking like a remnant from the last century as he watched his flock in that area of no fences. He was leaning on his stick just gazing, and thinking perhaps; about what, we shall never know, nor were we able to take a close photograph, but the memory remains and we would never have seen him by the main road, which is more to our present point.

All these facets of local life surely make up the enjoyment of visiting foreign places and enrich the time spent roaming around in search of secret vineyards. Although the lives of many of the wine-country's inhabitants are literally steeped in wine and its production, there is everyday life to be lived too, and if you take time to follow our recommendation and go off along the minor roads, you will find it; you might even be surprised to see how its pace differs from ours!

The signs to look for when on the track of vineyards whose owners will not mind your enquiry are as follows, and can be made more obvious sometimes by wrought-iron bunches of grapes hanging outside the house, or even mock bottles of wine, for instance, with the appropriate wording on the label.

vente directe	direct sale to the public
vente au détail	retail sales
propriétaire/viticulteur	owner/grower
dégustation	tasting
gratuite	free

These signs may be hung outside private houses. If you are in a little village and see a sign don't be put off if the place doesn't look very romantic or doesn't appear to be close to a vineyard, for proprietors often live a short distance away. These visits can often be the ones which lead to meeting people in their homes and staying much longer than the time it takes to taste the home produce. Signs can also be hung outside farm houses situated right in the middle of the vineyard, which has instant appeal, of course, for we feel as if we are seeing more of what is going on. The next chapter will tell of the variety of venues for tasting, so the rest of this chapter will offer advice and tips on how to locate your spot in the first place and how to have fun doing it.

There are perhaps three distinct methods of wine hunting. One is to have a very good idea of where you are heading, i.e. the village you wish to locate, and the kind of wine you want to try. To be in this position you must have either heard about the place from someone else, or you will have read about it, perhaps in the second half of this book where likely hunting ground is indicated. Sometimes a chance meeting with a local person can lead you off on the scent – the local baker could have recommended a friend of his up in the hills, or a waiter in a restaurant might tip you the wink and tell you where to get a good, cheap bottle, just as good, and half the price of what you are now drinking, *monsieur*. If you stay in the local *auberge*, or *en famille* at a small farm, you are sure to talk about your interest in wine and will be most likely overwhelmed with ideas on where to go to find it. Beware, however, of being sent to a tourist trap for, with the best of intentions, your host might think that this is the kind of thing you are looking for. Admittedly, with limited French, the thing takes a bit of explaining but if you employ your hands and expressions as well, you're sure to get somewhere!

Alternatively, you might simply be pioneering, having worked out that there must be something up this or that little lane, in view of all the terraced vines hanging from the slopes. We once spent half a day doing exactly this, in the Jurançon area, determined to take up the challenge and find some place other than the wine co-operative at Gan in the valley, even though we had heard it might be difficult, and everyone we asked directed us to those co-operative premises on the main road. Up into the hills we went and around endless hairpin bends into what must surely burst into vines at any moment, after all they were marked on the special map we were using. Well, we certainly knew that small area of the countryside intimately and enjoyed a picnic and some fine views before emerging once more at the same point, after a few false moves and swift three-point turns in people's drives, but we did not see a single vine, nor one *dégustation* sign!

A third method is to take potluck and hope for the best by heading off in a promising direction and making a pact with yourselves to stop at the first *dégustation* sign, whatever the place looks like. You can, of course, be lucky and have an enjoyable experience but, as at home when you buy an article on the spur of the moment without considering where the best selection or price might be, you are more likely to see the same thing at a better price shortly afterwards, or something more attractive at a similar price, and kick yourself. Take your time and enjoy discovering other things about the locality until you have got the feel of what it has to offer – then you can choose the place which has the most appeal.

If you are tracking down somewhere definite it is a good idea to have a Michelin map with you, but be warned, even a Michelin map cannot protect you against the dreaded French signpost. We have nearly come to blows, when one is driving and the other map-reading, and still we seem to pass the same tree or field twice and go round in ever-decreasing circles without locating the chosen spot. In open country, when you find yourself surrounded by vast tracts of identical looking vines well off the main roads, you can often travel for miles faithfully following the last signpost, wondering at the length of the French kilometre, until suddenly you find the next one and it is pointing you back again without your having seen a thing in between the two! Its all part of the game! Even in the élite district of Sauternes, where a well-signposted *route du vin* leads you through the interesting wine-producing area, signs can be encountered indicating the same place in two opposite directions, so we cannot blame ourselves, or even the crazy rural district council; to us it is just part of France, and the days when we find ourselves miles from where we intended to be usually end up with more interest in them than the ones which run according to plan.

On the subject of maps, I am reminded of one map in particular which served a purpose it could never have been designed for. It was one we picked up from the counter in a delicatessen and was simply an inaccurate picture map drawn for promotional purposes to tell the customer where all the local cheeses came from, this being a district in the lower Pyrenees. We knew where there was a grower of Jurançon wine (yes, we persisted a long time in looking for this one!) but had not found his village on our map. Incidentally, the address of the grower had come to our notice because we had read it on the label of a bottle in a wine-shop window, which shows that detective work can play a part in wine hunting. The cheese map miraculously had the name of the village on it where the grower lived – wonderful! We dutifully followed the cheese cartoons and arrows and managed to locate the village but there was no M. Guirouilh in sight, never mind his château, Clos Guirouilh, and it was only a small place. However, we accosted a local passer-by, feeling we had done well to get as close as this via a Pyrenean cheese route, and not wanting to be defeated again by this wine. He knew the place and it turned out to be a further six rural kilometres deep into the countryside, but the instructions were good and the place, when we eventually found it, provided us with one of our most memorable visits.

This little anecdote proves that discoveries can be made in the most unexpected quarters by unusual means if the would-be vineyard seeker has plenty of time and determination. The same story further serves to illustrate the point made about co-operatives, for although the Jurançon *moelleux* (sweet) was good at the co-operative at Gan, it was twice as good from M. Guirouilh, and a lot cheaper. Into the bargain the visit had been one of our best, so do take all these things into consideration when tracking down particular favourites of your own, it is well worth it in the end.

French road works can add variety to your day when you travel on the smallest roads in pursuit of wine. The locals, of course, know how to get to their destination by other routes, but alas for the poor, unsuspecting foreigner, map spread out on knee, finger glued to the spot! We spent several happy hours tracking down Château Chalon in the Jura to find out about its peculiar *vin jaune*, enjoying the pretty rural scenery, until the dreaded *déviation* signs appeared at the very last moment, just when Château Chalon village was in sight. No through road and no alternative suggestions, except to follow the first arrow and hope to see more in strategic places. We did, and drove several kilometres up and down dale, totally losing all sense of direction, even ending up among squawking chickens in someone's back yard, before approaching the place from an entirely new direction. We did, however, discover the local countryside and noticed that no-one else was offering this wine for sale, which made the whole journey worthwhile when we finally rolled up, minus a goodly amount of petrol at a delightful settlement perched on a hill, with views for miles around.

Not always will you find yourself chasing the best local wine, for sometimes there *is* no best, it is all much of one standard, and if this is what the area produces, then it is recommended that you try it. At one château in the Loire, we were trying several different types of wine, with some French customers, a fact which pleased us because it seemed to denote that the wine had a name for itself among the French themselves, not just the tourists, when a man arrived with plastic can in hand and gaily shouted, '*le plein, s'il vous plaît!*' This phrase is more normally heard on the garage forecourt, 'fill her up, please,' so we stared and watched as all good English tourists can, whilst his container was filled with one of the lower-quality wines from the list, which was nevertheless perfectly good for everyday drinking. The price was most advantageous compared with the same wine in bottles, and was sold by the litre. Why should the visitor not do this too? We recommend that you pack a couple of plastic water carriers with you when intending to track down wine, and be like the French. When in Rome, do as the Romans do. It will be useful for your picnics and evening relaxing and need not be brought home at all – to be consumed in situ! The words to look out for on the tariff or signboard are *vins en vrac*, loose wines. Do *not*, however, insult the growers who only have higher quality wine for sale by walking in jauntily with your container; it could give a bad impression, even if done in all innocence.

Whilst on the subject of impressions, we might mention here that you should take care not to give the idea that you are going to be important customers wanting to purchase several cases, particularly if you are in a poor rural district. It would be embarrassing when the time came for you to select your three bottles. If you look too prosperous you will stand out like a sore thumb against such farming background and

The pace of life differs at times from ours!

perhaps inhibit people from talking to you. At the other end of the scale, if you plan to visit one of the famous châteaux of Bordeaux, or take a guided tour of the wine-making areas, it's best to abandon your holiday shorts and funny tee shirts for a while – we know, much to our chagrin. There has been the odd occasion when we have visited a private domaine where the proprietor has glanced at our shorts and tennis shoes and rightly wondered whether we were likely to be potential customers or were simply interested in the free tasting offered. Usually these have been occasions when the visit was unplanned, but we have nevertheless felt uncomfortable in the tasteful surroundings we have often stumbled upon unwittingly, so do try to avoid this mistake.

The timing of your visit to a vineyard might be cause for some concern. In our English ignorance we used to think that early morning would not be a suitable time for wine-tasting, if only because at home we would not dream of drinking wine at that hour. But it can happen that you have arrived at your chosen spot the night before and want to move along when you have visited the vineyard first thing the next day. Suffice it to say that we have never been turned away on these occasions, but I would say that 10 o'clock would be the earliest to make enquiries, since people have their morning routines to get through before that, especially in farming areas.

Lunch hour, of course, is sacred and usually stretches between twelve and two. During this period the French take their midday break and it would be bad manners to expect them to answer their doors to you, so do respect the local customs, your visit will be far more welcome and therefore more enjoyable too. A good idea when out on your tour of vineyards is to time your own midday break to coincide with the local one and if it proves too long for your needs, the time can be profitably used by becoming familiar with the village nearest to your venue thus providing you with some talking point later, if your host or hostess seems ready to chat. Remember the advice in the earlier chapters; if people realise that you are indeed interested in their surroundings and work, they will be happy to make your visit as pleasant as possible.

What about evenings? Having arrived in Monbazillac one evening, with little else to do but take a walk after our meal, we wondered whether we dared approach the château we had lined up for the morning visit. Timidly, we made a sortie in our vehicle down its drive, to see whether it looked welcoming, and having decided everything was shut and no-one would want to be knocked up at that time of night, we crept away, hoping not to have been noticed. The following morning however, when we called and equally timidly asked the breezy old housewife in charge if it was not too early for wine-tasting, she simply said, of course not, why had we not knocked when we came last night? Accordingly, one night elsewhere at about 7.30, we braved a *chien méchant* who only wagged his tail in greeting, and on inquiring if it was not too late to taste wine, received the immediate reply, 'Of course not, it is never too late to discuss good wine.' We feel therefore that we can confidently recommend that the only time to avoid is the midday pause.

Asparagus and strawberries at a fair in the Loire

Whilst travelling in search of secret vineyards, keep your eyes open for notices of forthcoming events; this is a habit which can be cultivated most profitably and it goes hand in hand quite naturally with wine-hunting. The events referred to are those of a particularly local nature, events which you would not find advertised in the main tourist areas for they are not deemed worthy of great interest to outsiders. Sometimes it happens that you are not really sure what the event *is*, but if it says it starts at 10 o'clock in the village square, it's easy to find out. In this way, we first heard and later saw the strangest little band of musicians imaginable, all of them blowing on home-made red and yellow painted instruments, as far as we could make out, except for a drummer who tried unsuccessfully to keep it all together. As they puffed up a long flight of steps to the little street where we were waiting, intrigued, the noises became more disjointed and breathless and the tune distorted, but it remained with us for the whole of the day, because it was so catchy and simple. When the motley lot appeared they were all dressed in gay outfits and were drawn from the smallest boy to the oldest man. They were heralding something to do with sport, that was all we could make out from the poster, but for us it was a lovely start to the day, which we might easily have missed.

Particularly, look out for the word *foire*, for this one promises to be interesting. We arrived at a *boudin* or sausage fair once, having seen a notice and an arrow by the side of a very minor road we were using, and found it was to be a most colourful event as coaches containing costumed village groups rolled up ready for the start, many with brass instruments. The *boudins* seemed slow to appear however, so we had to move on and stumbled across a further *foire* completely by chance, having nosily followed a series of strawberry-shaped signs. That one turned out to be a joint strawberry and asparagus fair, both these items being the local speciality of the season. The goods were on sale but there was also a competition for the best design composed of the two products together, so here again was a chance to get a taste of local life and a few photographs too. At nearly all of these events there will be wine booths offering the native speciality, so what better way could you possibly combine your search for vineyards with an interest in local colour? Our red and yellow band was in the heart of the Vouvray wine region – one can only imagine what their music sounded like at the end of the day.

This kind of event will not magically turn up for you unless you are using the smallest of roads on your wine quests, so take a tip, when moving from one wine area to another, and use the minor roads roughly parallel to the main ones; above all, allow plenty of time for the unexpected stop, wine hunting is definitely not a hurried occupation.

THE
FIRST KISS

Let's imagine now that you have located a secret vineyard and are ready to knock on the door of a stranger – a French stranger. The prospect can be a bit daunting, it must be admitted, unless you are naturally brash and uninhibited. Particularly if this is the first time you have ventured away from the safe and anonymous tourist tasting spots, your mind might be assailed by a series of 'what ifs?', just as mine was the first time I was urged forward by my husband to take the plunge and knock. The job fell to me because I could speak some French, he said, but I'm not so sure that that was all there was behind his reasoning.

What if the person who opens the door does not look very welcoming? What if you don't like the look of them at all and wish you hadn't chosen the place, how can you extricate yourself from the situation? What if your few carefully rehearsed opening phrases escape you at this crucial moment, or worse still, what if that person comes out with an absolute torrent of rapid French, thinking you have understood every word and then pauses expectantly for your response? Finally, what if you try the wine and find it isn't any good, or you don't like any of it?

The last 'what if' is the easiest to answer, for you have already decided that this is the right area to try a certain type of wine, and you have been attracted here by the fact that you are pretty sure you will like it. The quality will be good, or the vigilant inspectors would be having something to say about things, and the wine should by law be whatever it purports to be on the label. If it is only a *vin de pays* you are trying and you have had no experience of it before, there might be some substance to the last question, but rest assured it should also be very cheap, so if courtesy compels you to buy a little, you can always cook with it if you are catering for yourselves, or give it away before you go home.

To go back to the first question. What if the person does not look very welcoming? Our own experience of knocking on doors is quite extensive now and only once have we been refused a visit. It was entirely our own fault because we had disturbed the household during the midday break, being new to wine discovering and not aware of the importance of the hour – apart from that, it was in Germany! The answer to the second question is really hard luck, once you have brought someone to the door you can hardly ask for a drink of water. You are committed once you have made this first move and we think its an exciting moment waiting to see what will happen, and what

kind of a tasting it will be, for no two are ever alike. If the sign for tasting, *dégustation* or *vente directe* is displayed, you can rest assured that the people will take time to be with you, so do forget your British reserve, take the plunge and enjoy yourselves!

Your secret vineyard could appear in many different guises, though it will not always have the romantic atmosphere that we all privately hope to find. Its 'secret' quality comes from the fact that it will not be seen by the tourist dashing through France on motorways and major roads; it does not advertise itself on hoardings nor in tourist brochures. You have to find it yourselves. Don't be put off by the austere or closed appearance of some premises. Often we have felt sure that there was no-one about, as all appeared so quiet and lifeless, but we have been proved wrong every single time. These properties are usually the older, well-established ones, often small mansions in themselves, and could have large courtyards and pleasant gardens surrounding them or have an imposing drive. Your reception at such an elegant dwelling will be just as friendly in its own way as that at a more humble abode, particularly if your own approach is courteous.

> *Drink no longer water, but use a little wine for thy*
> *stomach's sake and thine other infirmities.*
>
> TIMOTHY

If your carefully practised opening remarks desert you as the door opens and you are tongue-tied, you can at least murmur a greeting and '*dégustation,*' and the other person will soon help out. It cannot be emphasised too often how important it is to muster up as much French as possible, even if it is absolutely basic or totally without grammar, it will make such a difference to your reception. It simply does not matter whether you have come out with some terribly garbled expressions, because your host is far too polite to laugh or correct you and will have got the gist of your effort immediately.

It is amazing how well you can manage with lots of smiles and gestures when out on these expeditions, for if people *want* to communicate, they will find some means. When you have been greeted you will be led to whatever area is set aside for the purpose of receiving visitors for wine-tasting. Sometimes it is a cool parlour in the house itself, plainly decorated and furnished, often it can be a rather ornate room with beautiful antique furniture and fine-looking pictures on the walls, even in a house which from outside looked unassuming. Depending on the weather and season, you might be led into the courtyard or just on to a small patio with a sun umbrella for shade and comfort. Some growers like to equip a room, usually one of their outbuildings, with something that lends atmosphere to the place, such as dusty old bottles, upturned barrels to sit on, ancient vineyard artefacts, photographs of horses or oxen plodding through the vines. Wicker baskets for harvesting, trailing vines, lamp bases made of twisted old vinestocks, these and many other ideas are used to decorate the grower's tasting room and keep the visitor happy.

But often, in those places where few visitors are expected, or the *vigneron* is too busy with his work to think about anything else, it is to the cellar or the *chai* that you are led, his place of work. Here there is probably nowhere to sit and the glasses will still be dirty from the last time they were used; in other words the grower is not 'geared up' for tourist visits.

Let's imagine a typical tasting session inside one of the houses whose door you have dared to knock on. It is worthwhile having in your mind the type of wine you would be interested in trying, for it is nearly always the first question your host will ask you, if indeed he has a selection on offer. The most secret of secret vineyards will not have a selection, it will just be their current supply, but it's best to be prepared for all events. If you are not sure how to pronounce things or have no idea just what kind of a choice there is, simply ask for a wine list (*une carte*), it's always a useful dodge. Often you would be presented with one anyway, and given time to look at it while glasses are being brought or your host busies himself to let you have time to decide. You are at liberty to ask for several types, even if you have more or less already decided which one you might buy, in fact the more interest you show in them, the more pleased your host will most likely be, and he is sure to help you if you appear to need assistance. When there is more than one vintage to try and you wish to indicate the year of your choice, you can of course resort to pointing at the list, but as the wines on offer are only likely to go back to the mid-seventies, if that, why not mug up your French numbers for the seventies and eighties and be able to ask properly, its not much of an effort, after all, and will be a gesture. At this point, apologies to all proficient speakers of French – they must ignore these comments relating to effort – the only aim is to point out which phrases and figures are useful to help along the non-French speaker.

A typical wine list will usually begin with the cheapest bottle, and finish with the dearest, and if there are different styles of wine available they will often be put into groups such as dry, sparkling or sweet, to help you find your way about. Below are a few basic words you will find denoting the different categories, and the two wine price lists opposite will give you an idea of how they might be set out.

sec	dry	*blanc*	white
demi sec	semi-sweet	*rouge*	red
moelleux		*rosé*	rosé
liquoreux	sweet		
doux			
pétillant	sparkling	*marc*	spirits
mousseux			

Don't worry about the words which sometimes accompany each wine listed in the form of a brief description. Such words as *élégant* and *fine* can be guessed of course, but even then, we think that your own taste buds are going to tell you all you need to

price without tax, the column
for us! We pay on entering our own
country.

price with tax, for French people

wine price
list →

TARIF des VINS   du

«Domaine de Montmain»
Viticulteur
VILLARS - FONTAINE
21700 NUITS-ST-GEORGES
Tél. 80.62.31.94

note range
of wine →
styles on
offer

container wine,
i.e. 'loose'
wine, →

Appellation contrôlée	Millesime	Prix HT	Prix TTC	Caractère du vin
Bourgogne Aligoté (Blanc)	1985	21,92	26,00	Fruité, souple en bouche, typé
Bourgogne Rosé	1984			
Bourgogne Passetoutgrain	1984	21,07	25,00	Parfumé, accrocheur, aime à vieillir
Bourgogne Hautes Côtes de Nuits	1985			
Bourgogne Hautes Côtes de Nuits	1984	33,73	40,00	Léger, rond, élégant, doit vieillir 3 à 4 ans
Bourgogne Htes Côtes de Nuits Les Genevrières	1984	38,78	46,00	Assez tanique, fera bien dans 5 à 6 ans

comments
which help
the buyer
know when wine
is at its best for
drinking
←

Vin en vrac de septembre à fin décembre téléphoner pour connaître les disponibilités (rouge et rosé).

Champagne label language
(see p.116)

Février 1986

still Vouvray →

VOUVRAY TRANQUILLE

LE HAUT-LIEU

1984	Sec	31,00 F
1983	Sec	34,00 F
1985	Sec	38,00 F
1985	Moelleux	55,00 F

LE MONT

1980	Demi-Sec	33,00 F
1982	Sec	37,00 F
1985	Demi-Sec	45,00 F

name of one →
of the three
vineyards owned
by this grower

LE CLOS DU BOURG

1980	Sec	33,00 F
1983	Demi-Sec	34,00 F
1982	Demi-Sec	37,00 F
1985	Moelleux	65,00 F

TARIF VINS VIEUX, SUR DEMANDE

VOUVRAY PÉTILLANT

Brut	40,00 F
Sec	40,00 F
Demi-Sec	40,00 F
Cuvée Réservée Brut	45,00 F
Cuvée Réservée Sec	45,00 F
Cuvée Réservée Demi-Sec	45,00 F

← slightly sparkling
Vouvray

VOUVRAY MOUSSEUX
MÉTHODE CHAMPENOISE

Brut	40,00 F
Sec	40,00 F
Demi-Sec	40,00 F

← fully sparkling
Vouvray,
Champagne method

TOURAINE ROSÉ
MÉTHODE CHAMPENOISE

Brut	35,00 F
Demi-Sec	35,00 F

← Champagne
method, but
rosé of Touraine
AC used, not
Vouvray AC

conditions of →
sale; this part
does not normally
concern us

CONDITIONS DE VENTE

Ces prix s'entendent emballages perdus, droits de circulation et T.V.A. compris, nets sans escompte.
Paiement comptant à réception par chèque bancaire ou postal C.C.P. 265.15 L La SOURCE.
Conditionnement en cartons de 12 bouteilles, d'une ou plusieurs qualités, au choix du client.
FRANCO DE PORT POUR EXPEDITIONS EGALES OU SUPERIEURES A 24 BOUTEILLES.
PAR QUANTITÉ : de 60 à 96 bouteilles, remise 1,00 F par bouteille.
108 à 156 bouteilles, remise 2,00 F par bouteille. — Au-delà, nous consulter.
Ces conditions de Franco de Port et pour commandes par certaines quantités ne sont valables que pour livraison
à une seule adresse.

Tarif révisable en cas de changement de régime de taxe.

know. Taste in wine, after all, is a very personal thing, what gives pleasure to one person could well taste poisonous to another. The advice in this chapter is to taste at your own level and not pretend to be anything other than a wine-lover, unless of course you happen to be an accomplished taster. The following notes are aimed to help beginners so those with more experience must pass over them and read on. To be able to distinguish subtle nuances of flavour and bouquet, the palate and sense of smell must be trained; it is a question of learning a skill rather than being born with an ability. Wine experts must then be able to communicate what they experience when tasting, thus a wine-language has evolved which can be a source of amusement when such descriptions as the following are read: 'tight, closed-in bouquet which reluctantly yields scents of walnuts, *cassis*, leather, and of course cedary, herbaceous aromas,' or 'very grassy nose'. Every word of those two comments has real meaning and would communicate a 'sensory' experience to another person familiar with the procedure, but we are not going to become embroiled in all that. Those who wish to develop their tasting abilities will find books and courses available, but for our purposes, a few basic points should suffice.

Try not to do your tasting immediately after enjoying one of France's most pungent cheeses, or anything sour or vinegary which would leave a specific taste in your mouth. It is a good idea to eat a plain biscuit or two before a tasting visit as it clears away any previous tastes and provides something too, to soak up any heady liquid. Smoking during a tasting is definitely out as the smell would spoil any bouquet, and of course the taste of tobacco would overwhelm anything else such as 'grilled almonds', 'plums and violets' or 'barley-sugar and toffee', all of which descriptions appear regularly in wine-tasting notes.

Your host will first offer you the driest of your selection, just a small amount in a glass usually. In the course of our wanderings we have found that as a rule, the smaller the establishment, the further up the glass is your wine, so beware if you have shown interest in one or two different wines – it may happen that you need to leave some if the next offering is being pressed upon you, or if you are driving immediately afterwards. At one of our own very early tastings our host had gone to fetch glasses and we were congratulating ourselves on having penetrated a seemingly closed château in Germany, when I spotted a large glass bowl in the middle of the bar. All the comments we had ever heard about *real* wine-tasters in the trade came back to us, and I whispered to my husband that on no account was I going to *spit* into that thing – what a disgusting idea! We decided to swallow every drop of what was offered, however much there was and rather wished we had never entered that awesome place. You can imagine my relief when after joining us with the first glass, our host emptied the remains of his into the dreaded bowl and invited us to do likewise before continuing with something better.

You might be led into the courtyard . . .

Don't panic, therefore, about such unmentionable customs as spitting, for it doesn't come into your repertoire at all, it is strictly for those professional tastings when a large number of wines are being judged and most likely the wine is too young to be swallowed and enjoyed in any case. Nor do you need to slurp, gargle or roll your wine about in a ludicrous manner, simply take your time over the first mouthful and concentrate on what impressions you get. You could first of all look at the colour of the wine to see if it is clear, then swish it around to release its scents and smell the bouquet, maybe comparing notes with your companion about the smell. We noticed that the growers themselves, if they join you, take in some air when taking the first mouthful, making a slight noise, this action helping the wine to exude its flavours. Practise at home if you want to do this – it would be embarrassing to choke in public! Let the wine stay in your mouth a while, then, after swallowing, notice how long the taste remains with you; in general, a great wine's flavour will last a long time afterwards.

Above all, don't make an elaborate show of doing anything which doesn't actually mean anything to you; if you are a beginner at wine discovering, don't be afraid to say so, or to let it be seen. So long as you don't swig off your small glassful thoughtlessly your host will not mind in the least, and we have found he usually wants to help if he can, if you appear interested enough. At this point, your understanding of what goes into the growing and making of wine will stand you in good stead, for you might find references being made to sun, or soil, or cold weather, which will really mean something in relation to the wine you are trying, and it helps the session along enormously if you can appreciate something of what you are being told.

There are just two more facts to remember whilst we are on the subject of tasting. The first is connected with those wines which need to age a few years before their true potential is reached, such as Bordeaux. You might well be given a small amount from a first-year barrel to try, although this would only be a gesture on the part of the grower if he knows you are not a seasoned taster. My reason for saying this is that the wine is far too young to taste nice, it is only tasted at various stages of its maturation period to see how it is coming along, and to predict its potential for the future. These things are necessary to know for instance if that wine is being bought by a *négociant* in its early stages – he needs to have something to gauge his price by. Be ready, therefore, for an unpleasant taste and unless you have read round the subject and know what to look for in the flavour and bouquet, it's best to restrict your tasting to the one sip and to simply appear interested. Enthusiastic lip-smacking is definitely out; you will be seen to be the amateur you are if you display great signs of pleasure. The regional guide of this book will tell you how long the wines need to mature.

The other piece of cautionary advice is to do with the more expensive wines on offer. Your free tastings will cover the general wines up to a certain standard, but the grower will not be able to offer you his finest wine to try; you must judge from the progression of taste already experienced whether you would like to purchase any. Sometimes you might be lucky, as we occasionally have been, in that if a bottle of the more exclusive wine is open already, you might be allowed to try a little – the grower might even insist if he is enjoying your visit.

That is all you need to know about basic tasting procedure, but the real pleasure of a tasting session, we find, is when it develops into something more than just a *dégustation*. If the grower or his wife is enjoying meeting a couple of 'foreigners' your visit often turns into a family affair when the establishment is only a small one. We were once ushered into a small, spotless bungalow within sight of the owner's steeply terraced vines, but pointed out that we must first remove our heavy walking boots, for we were in the mountainous Savoie region. No need, gestured the lady, I haven't done any housework at all today yet, (the place was *gleaming* with polish and pin-neat), but since I was beginning to remove my boots despite this dubious remark, she brought out two pairs of enormous carpet slippers, designed for the working members of the family to slip over their boots, and in we shuffled, feeling rather self-conscious.

The slippers sealed our fate. One glass after another was poured in generous quantities, as broken conversation began to flow too amid many gestures, signs and laughs, until we had told each other all about our families, had given away our age after a direct question, and even ventured into our respective philosophies of life, finding we had much common ground. The only snag to all this was that there was no *bowl*. We were expected to drink up and be ready for whatever else *monsieur* our host wanted to share with us and I for one simply couldn't do it, partly because it was all far too dry for me to enjoy and partly because it was potent! Managing to extricate myself from a tricky situation by indicating that I was driving, and looking very serious about it, we sat in our slippers for a further hour and experienced one of our most pleasant expeditions.

This bungalow was not in the least a romantic-looking secret vineyard dwelling and had not at first looked very promising as far as interesting visits go, but it serves to show that appearances are deceptive and you never know what is going to result from your knock on the door.

Often after you have tasted the wines and made a purchase, you will be shown around the *chai* or building where the huge barrels are kept and be told about the work going on there, if you are interested; it all adds to your visit and proves that the grower too is enjoying telling you about his wine, for a *dégustation* does not need to include anything extra at all. A tasting session conducted in the *chai* itself is always interesting and can take several forms, from a brief and silent stand-up affair with the choice of two vintages, dirty glasses rinsed out on your arrival, to a group of people being taken from one barrel to another starting from the driest and progressing to the sweetest, these tastings usually being conducted at the larger places. In each case, your guide will use a *pipette*, a long glass tube to draw up the wine straight from the top of the barrel, and using his finger at the end, will release a little into your glass. It was through joining in one of these sessions that I discovered a rosé from Anjou that I wouldn't have asked to try normally, since we had been seeking the sweet white

Chaume wine of the Coteaux du Layon, but since we were all trooping from one barrel to the next, listening to our guide's description of what was in each, I took the opportunity since it was offered, and loved it. Those châteaux which offer a wide selection, such as that one in the Loire, are ideal places to make for if you are only intending to make the one stop in that district, for you can experience the whole range under one roof.

If, on the other hand, you fancy putting your tasting abilities to the test, and your staying power, a local wine fair is the thing to find. Here you have the opportunity to try to detect the subtle differences between the wine of one vineyard and another in close proximity to each other, a representative selection from each of a dozen or so estates being brought along to show off. This would be the equivalent of a horizontal tasting rather than the vertical one just described above, that is, you can try the same vintage of the same style of wine from several different châteaux and make your comparisons.

The fair we discovered at Rablay on the river Layon in the Loire was such a one and we stumbled upon it through being lost and confused by multiple *déviation* signs. It was 10Fr. to enter the street, our arms were stamped unceremoniously with something that didn't wash off, and a new experience began. The street was lined with stalls or booths, each one belonging to a grower within a radius of about fifteen kilometres, and consisting quite simply of a table top with a few glasses on it and several bottles already opened, cases of wine being stocked behind. One stall held a grand display of *pâté de foie gras*, also a local product, whose price was prohibitive to us, and the rest of the street was a sea of wine. It appeared that there had been a judging of all the vineyards there, for we arrived just in time to hear a grand announcement after a boring (because we didn't understand it) speech and a fanfare of brass upon the makeshift stage. Wherever an event takes place, whatever it is, the French will provide a brass band for the occasion, or so it seems.

There was a surge of men towards one particular booth and toasts were drunk to the health of its owner, much to our gratification, because we had already bought something from him without knowing that he was a likely contender for the *médaille d'or*. The fair was to celebrate the coming of age of the latest vintage and was probably a trade fair as much as anything else, i.e. hoping to attract bulk purchasers from further afield; it was certainly not for tourists for it was only mid-May. A very welcome stall provided sausages and bread which rapidly becomes necessary after several ports of call at such affairs, and there was a fascinating exhibition of old vineyard machinery.

Particularly because this was not a tourist or holiday attraction, it was interesting to note that for a further 10Fr. you could go into a marquee and take a short course on wine-tasting. This then was for the local people, all of whom would be familiar with wine, so it denoted to us that there is still plenty to be learnt even in the case of those who are well-used to it, and they obviously didn't mind admitting the fact.

A wine fair thus provides an opportunity to try the produce of a dozen or so vineyards, without doing any travelling or map-reading in between and can obviously be a very educational as well as pleasurable experience, all for 10Fr.! I must admit that to me it all tasted equally wonderful, being the good '83 vintage and to my taste anyway, but had we ventured into the marquee, I feel sure that under guidance, and tasting one wine closely followed by another, even I would have begun to perceive slight differences.

A local wine festival is well worth seeking out since you cannot rely on the luck we had in stumbling across one, and we think it a good idea to make enquiries on arrival in your holiday or touring area, so that you can then work your trip around it and not be disappointed to find you have just missed one. A word of warning about buying from wine festivals, however. If the event is a large, well-organised whole day or weekend one, with plenty of added attractions taking place in a huge marquee, the chances are that it takes a great deal of money to stage and organise, thus the wines you can buy there are more highly priced than at the home or premises of the grower.

The best idea is to enjoy the events and have a few glasses of this and that, but then take note of whose wine you liked, for the names should be displayed, and track them down the following day. It's all part of the detective work and great fun. The wines at our street fair were all priced the same, virtually, and were exactly what was also being charged on the estates.

A few words need to be said now on the subject of buying as opposed to tasting wine. Naturally the words *dégustation gratuite* look most inviting but I am sure they are not meant to be taken absolutely at face value. Yes, there is no charge for the tasting session, but of course it is implied that you will be purchasing something at the end of the day. The question which first of all might come to your mind when you have discovered a wine or wines you would like to buy, is how many am I expected to buy? If you are touring and likely to stop at several other places en route, you could rapidly accumulate a large number of bottles for taking home which, first of all, take up space in your vehicle and, secondly, need to be checked out at the customs shed in England. You might also be limiting yourself on how much money you are spending on this part of your holiday.

Most *dégustation* places have cardboard cartons at the ready, with the name of their château or the general wine of the area printed on them, to hold three, six or twelve bottles, so it could safely be said that three would be an acceptable minimum. Those three could be all the same label or you could choose three different kinds. If you know in advance that you are going to buy only three bottles of something, my advice is to keep your visit fairly brief; it doesn't seem fair to occupy your host's attention for any great length of time if the resulting sale is to be quite modest. Of course, if after you have made your request, your host is still happy to chat and show you things, that is a bonus and gives you in turn the opportunity to compliment him on his industry, his family, or just anything you can manage to convey with sincerity. This is the part of the visit which we value most, the meeting with people and the chance to hear about their way of life.

A second question which could arise is, 'How am I to choose between the various wines which I liked?' We have decided not to give vintage guides for various reasons which are set out in the next chapter, so here our advice is to ask the grower his opinion when you find yourself in a dilemma. Naturally, you will narrow your selection down to what appeals to *you*, not him, but when a further choice is to be made, he is the one to help. We have always found people absolutely honest and fair in this respect and can think of several occasions when help was gratefully received. In Cahors at a rather impersonal château, we nevertheless were helped by the young estate worker who offered us the tasting, for when asked which vintage was better to choose, the '78 or the '79, he replied immediately to the effect that for one franc more, the '78 was a better buy, for the '79 was '*en déclin.*'

At Château de Barbe, on the opposite side of the Gironde to Bordeaux, we found we could not taste anything as there was no wine *chambré*, or at room temperature ready for offering, it being rather early in the season for visitors dropping in. That young man could have fobbed us off with a bottle to try that was not at a suitable temperature, and pressed us into a sale, but he didn't. Instead of that he answered our questions about vintages and advised that '81 had the greatest potential for his particular vineyard, though not perhaps for the whole of Bordeaux. He also dissuaded my husband from treating himself to a '69 which he had mistakenly thought to have been a good vintage, even though he would have benefited from the sale. We were impressed with this kind and honest service. A further example to illustrate the fact that the man on the spot knows best is provided by this same gentleman, who was very much an expert in his own field and well educated in wine-lore in general. When asked by us about the Sauternes vintages, he shook his head and said we must ask the growers there, one simply could not generalise.

Two questions to ask yourself when selecting wine to purchase are, firstly, for what purpose do I want this wine, and secondly, will I be able to transport it home without spoiling it?

If you want the wine for immediate use and everyday purposes, it is likely that you will not be paying a great deal for it. Remember, however, that all wines are subject to the same amount of duty regardless of quality and price paid, so if it seems that the duty to be paid will make your cheap wine seem too dear for its purpose, it might be better just to enjoy that one whilst you are travelling around and pay a bit extra for a better quality one to bring home.

Some wines are intended to be kept a long time and are called *vin de garde* – Bordeaux, Sauternes and some of the Loire sweet wines are in this category. If you want to purchase some *vin de garde*, with which to stock up your cellar for the future, do ask your host about which year is likely to be a good one; he will be pleased to be consulted and to see that you do not intend to toss off his precious wine without a thought for leaving it until it is at its very best. Our friend at the Château de Barbe told us quite plainly that even when you have studied oenology and been in the wine-making business for years, a wine can still bring surprises; you can never really know what it will be until the ageing process is complete.

The second question, that of transportation, is relevant to *vins de garde* in particular. Some of them have sediment in the bottom of the bottle, which if possible should not be mixed with the wine, particularly in the case of 'heavy reds'. Some need an even temperature to be able to continue the work the vintner has begun. We were advised against the '69 Bordeaux my husband was hankering after because it was a poor year in that district, but even had it been a good year, it was a bad idea, for it would have been jolted up and down in our vehicle during the rest of our energetic holiday in the mountainous regions to the south. During the day it would have its temperature raised by the sun pouring through the vehicle windows, and the nights where we were heading at that time of the year would be very cold. Not a good idea! One only has to consider all the time, knowledge, worry and hard work which goes into the making of a fine wine, to put oneself in the grower's shoes and inwardly weep with him at the sight of thoughtless or blissfully ignorant tourists with money to spare making off with the fruits of his labour jolting and jostling among their camping equipment in the car boot. A young wine of good potential travels much better than an older one nearing the end of its life.

Many of the vineyards offer an *expédition*, or export service, which enables you to send in an order and have wine shipped off to you under reasonably good conditions. Of course, you would need to buy in a certain quantity to make this worthwhile and you would obviously need to be sure about the quality of the wine you were ordering, but for those who don't or can't get over to France each year, it's one other way of buying your wine from your own private source, even at long distance.

To recap on the subject of the last couple of chapters, the accent is on individuality. From the start to the finish of discovering wines at source from France's secret vineyards, you are in absolute charge of the operation yourself, you are not swept along on a tide of tourism. *You* choose your wine region, *you* go hunting for a likely tasting venue; it will be a highly individual character who has grown the grapes for the wine you will eventually choose. The choice will be made according to *your* individual taste, with no outside pressure of advertising or business interests to channel you into choosing what people want you to have. It's up to you too to get the most out of your tour and feel that you have really done something on holiday, instead of ambling about aimlessly and wondering why nothing ever happens to you, as it seems to in the case of others when you compare holiday notes. Make it happen! Become familiar with the surroundings you find yourselves in, show a real interest in the people in the *pays de vignoble* and things will happen of their own accord.

Bonne chance!

GETTING THE TASTE

Perhaps it is not the intention of every wine-loving traveller in France to bring back cases full of wine to store away at home, but if you have visited several châteaux, domaines or farmhouses, the chances are that you will have bought more wine than you needed for holiday consumption – this is always a delightful problem. The more inquisitive or interested a traveller you are, the more likely are you to want to buy, especially after long and entertaining visits with friendly, generous people. Most of us, too, like to bring back a souvenir in the form of something expensive to put away for a special occasion. Some visitors to France might have the express purpose in mind of buying wine there in order to stock up their cellars at home, and how much more interesting a method this will be than relying on a wine merchant at home to provide those needs.

Whichever category you fall into, it can be safely assumed that there will be some 'extra luggage' in your vehicle which may or may not be enjoying the trip as much as you. If you have bought wine which you intend to drink in the few months following your return home, it should be of the kind which requires no special care and travels well. Also, it is hoped, you will have taken note of my advice and not selected the cheapest or most ordinary ones you tasted, for they will simply not be worth the customs duty. If you chose, however, something which will not be immediately ready to drink, you need to know how to care for it once you have got it safely home. It would be a great shame to ignore this aspect and spoil what was otherwise a good purchase.

The present-day British customs duty rules permit a choice for the returning traveller so that if you do not have any of the fortified wines or spirits among your goods, you can bring in a few more bottles of still wine duty free. Perhaps this is worth considering when weighing up whether you intend to go over the limit, or indeed by how much. Make a point of collecting a leaflet describing the duty rules on your outward journey so that you avoid unnecessary shocks when arriving back with creaking axles.

When deciding how much wine to bring home with you, do bear in mind all those comments in the first chapter which refer to the generally limited selection of imported wines available to us and the often low-quality bracket into which they fall. When a fairly ordinary bottle of French wine costs you £3 to £4 from a retail outlet at home, its character having nothing much to distinguish it, and you can find a really good wine from its local source which still costs less than those mundane ones, even with duty added on, you don't need to ask the question whether or not it is worthwhile bringing some home. It is really only a question of how much you can afford at the time, and how soon you might be returning to replenish your stocks.

Let's assume that you bring sufficient bottles back with you to last a few months at least, and among them you have some which must not be opened for some years to come. If you make a habit of doing this with every opportunity which arises (and we rather think that wine-hunting can become addictive), you will need to make special storage arrangements at home. Most homes nowadays do not have cellars built below them, so unless you are one of those lucky people who live in an older house and have a ready-made room to receive your trophies from abroad, alternatives must be organised.

There is no real mystery or technique involved in the care of wine; it simply needs to be kept at a cool, even temperature and in the dark. For most of us, a cupboard will suffice, though specialist shops will show you their range of thermostatically controlled storage units if you are interested. These latter have certain drawbacks, so approach with caution and don't be carried away by an enthusiastic salesman who doesn't know as much about wine as he does about cold storage.

The very best of vineyards is the cellar.
BYRON

Having located a cupboard and ejected what was previously in it, (my jams, pickles and preserves were all turfed out unceremoniously into the spare bedroom!) make sure it is nice and clean and then eye it up for size and possibilities. Wine needs to be stored on its side so that the cork can be kept moist; if this is not done there is a danger that the cork will dry up and shrink, possibly letting in air eventually and spoiling what you are hoping to keep for several years. Those bottles which you must discipline yourself to leave alone to mature need to go towards the back of the cupboard, for they must not be disturbed at all. They can be left in the original cardboard box so long as there is no dampness around.

Apart from the cardboard boxes, you can use racks and will find a variety of these on offer in many shops, or you can make your own kind of arrangements using thin pieces of wood to separate the layers of bottles. Bottles can be simply 'binned' on their sides, one on top of the other, which doesn't take up much space, but it would prove quite difficult if you wanted to extract one from the bottom of the pile! Make sure that you can see what the bottles are by letting the labels show and having the capsules facing outwards.

All you need to do then is put the right wines in the right places, your maturing ones to the back with a 'do not disturb' notice on them, and your 'drink now' ones in

an accessible position. An important point to remember is that your wine needs to rest after its travels before being at its best again for drinking, so leave it about a month before attacking it. We have found it great fun and even necessary these days to keep our own cellar book which sounds rather grand but isn't. Whatever your own level of wine buying and whatever your taste, even if you only bring back a few bottles each visit and don't keep them for long, a cellar book can read rather like a holiday diary. If on the other hand you are becoming an addict, you will certainly need your book to keep you straight, in that it will remind you where each bottle is kept and when you should be checking to see if it is ready to drink.

These books can be purchased, but we think it much better to buy a suitably sized book and make up your own, according to the kind of things you would like to have in it. The following shows two typical entries taken from our book:

NAME	YEAR/GRAPE	WHERE BOUGHT	QUANTITY	PRICE	DRINK BY	NUMBER	COMMENTS
Château le Bartadis	'70	Monbazillac (M. Gazzin)	6, top left	29 Fr.	No rush		Avec foie gras, Ooh la la!
Coteaux de Layon	'69 Chenin blanc	Rablay fair, 83	One, in stock	80 Fr.	Keeps 20 years	gone '86	Cork blew out! Refermentation YUK!

From this record, we know exactly which grower it came from, its price, how many we bought and where we put them. We have made our own note of when to drink it, knowing how long Sauternes-style wine can keep, and so far, as can be seen from the blank space in the number column, we have left it alone. The final comment means nothing to anyone else, but for us that phrase is all we need to recall what fun and games there were during that visit. The lady managing the sales area made the above comment when we asked her what the '70 was like, since it was not on offer for tasting, but the way in which she said it was just so utterly French that it beggars description.

For some of you the comments column will serve as a space for tasting notes, so that you can refer to it later, having perhaps forgotten what it was like, and decide whether you would like to buy something else of that style if it was particularly good and you have the chance of a further visit.

Our particular book divides into a number of wine-producing countries and sub-divides into the major areas of France and Germany, the two we visit most often. If some of the labels are very attractive, or if we happen to have a 'rare' or 'famous' one, my husband soaks it off and fixes it into the book, to serve as a reminder and make the pages interesting. Not every purchase you make is a wise one, as can be seen by the second entry (*above*), taken from our Anjou section! Our comment reveals that we do not go in for wine language, we have our own expressions, but it serves to remind us of the fair we visited in '83 and perhaps it tells us that our '69 Coteaux du Layon did not like travelling round France in a camper van. It also provides me with an opportunity to say, 'I told you it wasn't worth paying all that for!'

A cellar book can be a serious or light-hearted affair or as with us, a mixture of the two, but it certainly is a good method of keeping a record if you decide to devote more time and money to stocking up your personal cellar. The 'drink by' column is a particularly important one, hence our earlier recommendation that you make a note of your grower's advice when purchasing. Drinking a wine before it is ready or leaving it until it is past its best is just a waste of the grower's time and your money.

All that remains now is to enjoy your wines once you have got them safely home and stored. Good wine deserves the right glasses, and although there is a variety of shape and size designed to suit the qualities of particular styles of wine, the plain tulip-shaped glass will meet all purposes, with its slightly incurving rim to gather up the bouquet.

If you decant your wines before use, even your more 'common' ones, and let them thus breathe a while, you will notice a difference in bouquet and flavour compared with that which is poured straight from the bottle. We discovered this fact for ourselves by accident, and have decanted all our wines ever since; besides, it's an excuse to have an attractive decanter on the table! The younger wines, especially, benefit from this method, for the oxygen contained in them has not yet had a great deal of time to make its effect felt on the wine. Decanting, of course, solves the problem of any sediment getting accidentally poured out with a wine and looking unsightly in the glass. The bottle which contains sediment should be held horizontally, after the cork has been removed as smoothly as possible, then poured in one movement until the sediment appears in the neck. Remember to do this a few hours before you require the wines and you will reap the benefit; it is not a question of being over-fussy, simply a matter of getting the very best out of them.

Another factor to take into consideration for the same reason is the temperature at which you serve your wine. Sometimes the bottle you choose will have advice written on it, usually around the neck-label, such as *servir frais*, or serve chilled, but when there is no such advice, its a good idea to follow the general rule of serving white wines cool but not ice-cold, and full-bodied reds at room temperature, for which the French word is *chambré*. We heard an appalling story recently via an acquaintance. He once stayed with very wealthy clients of his in America who employed a butler and were used to having the best of everything, including wine. One evening the butler came in to announce to his employer that he had prepared the wine thoroughly, it had been in the fridge for four hours and was now ready. Imagine our friend's horror when he sat to table and saw what the wine was – Château Mouton

Rothschild 1947, ice cold and dripping in water! He cupped his hands around his glass as often as he dared during that meal in order to try and salvage something of the wine's flavour, but alas it was useless. His host and hostess had absolutely no idea how to serve their magnificent wine and he was too much of a gentleman to say anything. The leaflets which growers often have to give you with your purchases will give specific information on the subject of temperature, but there is always scope to experiment and see what your own preferences are.

Some wines go well with food, others are much better appreciated on their own so that the full aroma and taste can be experienced without being confused by other sensations. Again, the choice is a personal one, so don't think you must follow other people's advice on this point, though certain common sense factors rule out some combinations immediately. A red-hot curry would completely obliterate the finer nuances of a delicately perfumed sweet wine for instance, whilst a rather bland-tasting fish dish would be helped along by something with a strong dry character. Specific rules about which wines to serve with which foods are to be ignored in our opinion; common sense and your personal taste will come into its own here.

If more than one wine is to be served with a nice long dinner for guests, a careful consideration for which order they are served in will avoid wasting any of the extra-special qualities which particular ones possess. Young before old, white before red, light before full-bodied, dry before sweet; those are fairly safe guidelines. A glass should never be filled right up to the brim, for this gives people no opportunity to enjoy the full bouquet by swirling the wine round gently. Lest you be thought mean by your guests, have fairly large glasses so that a two thirds measure is still generous.

The only thing left to do now is sit back and thoroughly and unashamedly enjoy your wine to the full, and you will find that your experiences of tracking down France's hidden wines will come to life again as soon as someone says, 'Where did this one come from?' Then comes your chance to reveal your private sources and encourage others to take an adventurous step or two away from the main roads and discover for themselves the unlimited wealth and variety of France's secret vineyards.

(*Overleaf main picture*) The medieval part of Nérac by the river. (*Inset left to right*) Pyrenean cheeses with their maker in his cellar; the grapes have ripened but are they ready to pick? Just south of the Muscadet region is the Vendée, home of these tempting brioches

Part Two
THE WINE REGIONS

INTRODUCTION

Main towns and rivers are shown so you can relate these guide maps to a Michelin, or other good map, from which you can select your own route between chosen stopping places. Wine-producing regions are shaded in, and limits for each separate appellation are shown by a dotted line. The heavy shading indicates where wine production is concentrated most, or where it is considered to be at its best in that region. This presentation by no means rules out the possibility of finding good quality, interesting wine in the lightly-shaded areas, however; it could be that such an area is spread over a large district with small concentrations dotted about in many different places, as in the case of the Entre-deux-Mers in Bordeaux, or the Minervois and Corbières regions of the Languedoc, for example.

Villages or towns in whose area there are plenty of private producers ready to sell their wine are plotted on the maps, and where well-known or famous châteaux and vineyards exist, they are keyed into the map by number. The absence of this feature denotes that either it is an area of co-operatives or, more likely, that there are plenty of good estates but none considered sufficiently outstanding to be shown.

A good, large-scale map of your own will be necessary if you intend to take wine hunting seriously, for many of the smaller villages mentioned are simply not on the average touring map and require you to locate tiny side roads. If map-reading is not your forte, the local *Syndicat d'Initiative* or Tourist Information Bureau often has leaflets prepared for wine seekers with easy-to-follow wine routes marked on them relating to the nearest vineyard. Many of these regions also have *routes de vin* clearly signposted around the villages, which at least help you to get near enough to your goal to ask directions. We have been amazed at times to find that all the wine-growers seem to be known for miles around, even in out-of-the-way districts where no-one appears to have made a name for themselves, and have been overwhelmed occasionally by the degree of help offered for finding someone. Several times people have simply said, 'Oh, it's quite near here, but you'll never find it, follow me,' and have proceeded to lead us to the door in their vehicle, often going out of their way to do so. A good tip is to have your address and the grower's name printed on a piece of paper which you can then show someone – your pronunciation and his may not always coincide!

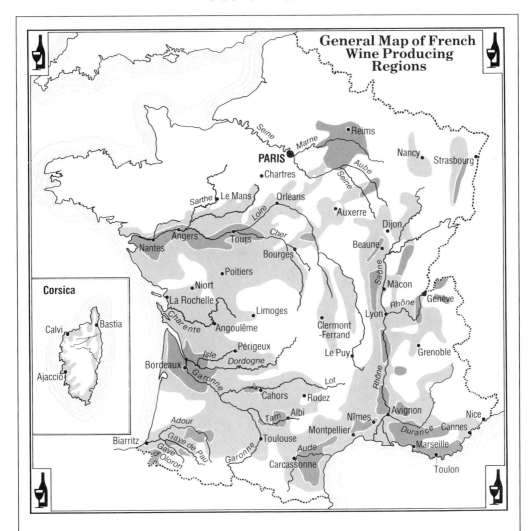

General Map of French Wine Producing Regions

Seine
Marne
Reims
PARIS
Nancy
Strasbourg
Chartres
Aube
Sarthe
Le Mans
Orléans
Seine
Auxerre
Loire
Dijon
Angers
Tours
Cher
Beaune
Nantes
Bourges
Saône
Poitiers
Mâcon
Niort
Genève
La Rochelle
Limoges
Rhône
Lyon
Charente
Angoulême
Clermont-Ferrand
Grenoble
Périgeux
Isle
Le Puy
Dordogne
Bordeaux
Rhône
Garonne
Lot
Cahors
Rodez
Tarn
Albi
Nîmes
Avignon
Nice
Adour
Montpellier
Durance
Cannes
Biarritz
Gave de Pau
Toulouse
Marseille
Gave d'Oloron
Garonne
Aude
Carcassonne
Toulon

Corsica

Calvi
Bastia
Ajaccio

LOCAL HISTORY

The local history of the region is related at the beginning of each section to put you into the picture. You may find that a little advance background knowledge of this nature can help enormously when arriving in a new area; you can often relate what you are seeing to some important aspect of history which influenced the evolution of the vineyard where you are. Many growers will stock leaflets, *(dépliants)*, which are designed to be given out to interested parties, so don't hesitate to ask; they usually begin with a potted history of their area and are often in English as well as French. Most of them give details of grapes used, what temperature is recommended for serving the wine and which dishes go well with it.

GRAPE VARIETIES, OR CÉPAGES

You will find a list of the grape varieties used in the making of each type of wine, but remember also to look at the type of terrain the plants are grown on, for the resulting wine gains its characteristics from the interaction between the two. Beware of judging one variety in one specific area and thinking that it will give a similar wine in all areas, for nothing could be further from the truth. The Gamay of the Beaujolais, for example, is ideally suited to what it finds under the surface there, but is flatly ruled out as being unacceptable in many other areas. Included in this section will be many unusual varieties which grow only in one very small area; you will find that their growers are particularly proud of this fact and will want to tell you about it.

VINTAGE GUIDES

After much deliberation it was decided not to give any vintage guides in this book, for several reasons. Firstly, as is usually pointed out in all the other wine books, they can only be used tentatively 'as a general guide' for there are always so many exceptions where freak conditions did something special for one region, or a grower excelled himself, etc. that they can be quite misleading. When an area is huge, such as Bordeaux for instance, it would need several such guides for all the separate appellations, since a general one would be quite useless in some places. A grower in St-Émilion this year gave us a little vintage guide, with his address printed on the reverse, but told us not to bother using it for it wasn't any help for widespread areas and individually talented growers. We agree with him.

Secondly, most of the vintage guides available tend to be more suitable for using in conjunction with the wines of the important châteaux, whereas this book is concentrating rather on those of *petits châteaux* and small family estates. The information will not be applicable generally, for the smaller places tend to make wine of less stature.

A further reason for the exclusion of vintage charts has to do with the fact that, over the last few years, wine technology has become more advanced and more widely

available to all, with the result that the general standard of all French wine is very high. Any wine which has not been found to be of the appropriate quality for its status will simply not be on sale as such.

A final reason, which convinced us that vintage charts are not necessary here, is that the last few years have all been very good, particularly '83, '85 and '86, and since it is wine of recent vintage that we recommend you buy, you can be sure that it will be good.

However, the aim of this book is to be helpful, particularly to the newcomer to wine-discovering, so instead of a rule of thumb, 'phony' vintage chart, sound advice is offered as follows:

1   Ask your grower after you have tasted his wines whether they are to drink now or to lay down a year or so. The most simple French for this would be *à boire?* and *à garder?* respectively. If the wine is to keep, ask him *combien d'années?* how many years? though he is sure to tell you without much questioning on your part.

2   If you'd like to check whether a year was good, just say *une bonne année?* with a question mark on your face, and take things from there. The growers are used to 'foreigners' and are usually delighted to communicate by some means or other if you are having difficulties.

3   Look at the price list. The wine the grower judges to be his best will have the higher price after it.

These few points should help you choose your wine without any worries about whether you are doing the right thing or getting good value. Trust the grower, for we have never met an unhelpful one yet on our travels.

ADDRESSES

The object of this book is, admittedly, to encourage the wine-lover to seek out his or her own supplier, but just one address is given for each main wine type, in order to help those who are perhaps bewildered at the choice in some places, a little concerned about whether they will pick a 'good' one, or just do not have the time to spend looking for one if enjoying other activities too. We have visited each address given and can guarantee good wine to be on sale with a pleasant, friendly reception, the latter being as important as the former, for us at least. The venues will vary from small and unknown to the fairly large and well-known. If in the latter category, they have been chosen because other places are difficult to find, because the quality of wine elsewhere is uncertain, or because there is some special point of interest there for the visitor.

An address is given at the end of each chapter to which you can apply for further information required, e.g. touring possibilities, *gîtes*, camping, outdoor pursuits and accommodation. Mention your particular needs when writing, and the appropriate areas you wish to visit, and you will receive the necessary details and brochures to help with the advance planning of your visit.

REGIONAL PRODUCTS

Products of the regions, such as honey, cheeses, and special dishes, will be mentioned but will be by no means exhaustive; this section is just designed to whet your appetite. Similarly, places of particular interest will be pointed out when within reach of wine venues.

FOOTNOTE

Readers may be surprised to see that some well-known areas with great wines are given less space than others which are relatively unknown. The reason for this is that we would like to encourage wine-lovers to find out more about the little-known wines instead of always heading for the safe and familiar, tried and tested over the centuries. Some vineyards have histories and reputations reaching beyond those of the well-known ones and have sadly diminished in size, but our recent travels have proved that they are very much alive and thriving and we are therefore bringing them to your attention.

It will be noted, too, that detailed descriptions of wines to be found are not given. This is deliberate, in the belief that the enjoyment of wine is a subjective pleasure; readers will like to make up their own minds about perfumes, tastes and sensations. The basic types of wine produced will be set out clearly in each chapter but the rest is up to you! Two friends independently judged a wine of ours to smell of rotting cabbages, though enjoying its taste, whereas the description in a reputable wine book was 'honey and flowers' – this incident serves to illustrate the point made.

ALSACE

The geographical position of Alsace and its history are inextricably entwined and can be held jointly responsible for the wines we know today as typical of this area. The Vosges range of mountains separates it from the rest of France and much of it lies within a dozen or so miles of the river Rhine.

A brief outline of the history of this colourful part of France, for those who have forgotten, will add to your appreciation of its wines and how they differ from those of the rest of the country. Alsace has been tossed about and bargained for between France and Germany since the Franco-Prussian war in 1870 when Germany claimed it and kept it until the First World War. During that time its prolific wines were used to strengthen the lighter German ones. Reclaimed by France after 1918, Alsace began to revive and improve its vineyards by replacing the 'common' vines with what the wine trade call 'noble' varieties, with quality rather than quantity in mind. No sooner had the results of these labours begun to become apparent than the Second World War broke out, German rule began again and Alsace suffered untold damage to both vineyards and property. She recovered gradually after the war, carefully rebuilding towns and vineyards, and today remains firmly French and proud of it, but the wine as a result of all these happenings has become highly individual, neither wholly French nor wholly German-style.

Although the soils, climate and grapes are very similar to those of nearby Germany, the Alsace method of wine-making brings about a totally different finished product. The produce is fermented until it is absolutely dry, unlike the German wine made across the border – the famous, delicate wines of the Mosel and the great sweet wines of the Rhine. Nearly all Alsace wines are very dry, highly flavoured, and strong in alcohol content, to say nothing of their noticeably heady bouquet. Students of geology would be interested to work out how this long, narrow strip of land contains so many different types of terrain, even within the one commune, but suffice it to say that it is this factor which allows us to find several different grapes being used to make several totally different wines which we can taste at the one venue.

GRAPE VARIETIES
Sylvaner
Pinot Blanc (or Klevner)   Tokay Pinot Gris
Riesling   Gewürztraminer
Muscat d'Alsace   Pinot Noir

In Alsace the grape variety has added interest, for it is that which features on the label in large letters, rather like the château, domaine or vineyard used elsewhere in France. When ordering a glass of wine with your meal, you would ask for Sylvaner or Riesling for example, unless you were going to enjoy the house carafe wine which will be an Edelzwicker, a blend of various varieties, which is very good straight from the barrel. As with the Grüner Veltliner from Austria, this wine is at its best drunk young and fresh and loses its character the minute it is bottled.

The Pinot Noir is the only red or rosé wine, all the others being white. The Muscat might bring surprises for the newcomer to Alsace, for it is not at all the sweet wine we are accustomed to of that name in other regions, yet it is the Gewürztraminer and Riesling which attract the most attention generally. Gewürz is German for spice, spiciness being an unmistakeable quality of this grape. Apart from the scent of the wine, which is very specific, its strength of flavour is what is most remarkable and it remains with you long after you have left your tasting venue. This is the wine most people associate with Alsace, especially in conjunction with its rich cuisine, but it is the Riesling which the Alsatians consider their greatest, having more hidden subtleties to explore than the instantly appealing (or non-appealing, according to taste,) Gewürztraminer.

Much of Alsace's wine is handled by giant firms such as Hugel, Dopff and Irion and Preiss-Zimmer which tend to have smart-looking shops in the most popular tourist towns, or by co-operatives, for many growers in this area have only a small patch of vines which they tend perhaps in their spare time and they sell their harvest to the latter as it is not worth their while to buy the expensive equipment needed for vinification. There are hundreds of private growers however, each with their *propre récolte* or *propriétaire/viticulteur* sign displayed, so there is absolutely no problem in selecting your Alsace wines to take home. Better still, it is the custom of many growers to display their bottles outside the property, often with prices attached, a German rather than French habit, which helps the prospective tourist enormously. A well marked wine route connects all the best villages and many vineyards have been provided with *sentiers*, or paths, with helpful notice boards at intervals to explain the work involved out there.

Before finding a tasting venue, have a look at the bottles in the shop windows with a view to becoming familiar with the labels, for Alsace does not slot neatly into the pattern which France's wine laws have established elsewhere. Below are a few words or expressions appearing on the labels and their explanation:

Mise d'Origine – by law, all Alsace's wine is bottled in Alsace.
Crémant d'Alsace – a sparkling wine, made by the Champagne method.
Grand Cru – certain specific vineyards or slopes are now being officially recognised as being outstanding by having their own AC conferred on them. They have always been in existence but Alsace is just beginning to 'conform'.

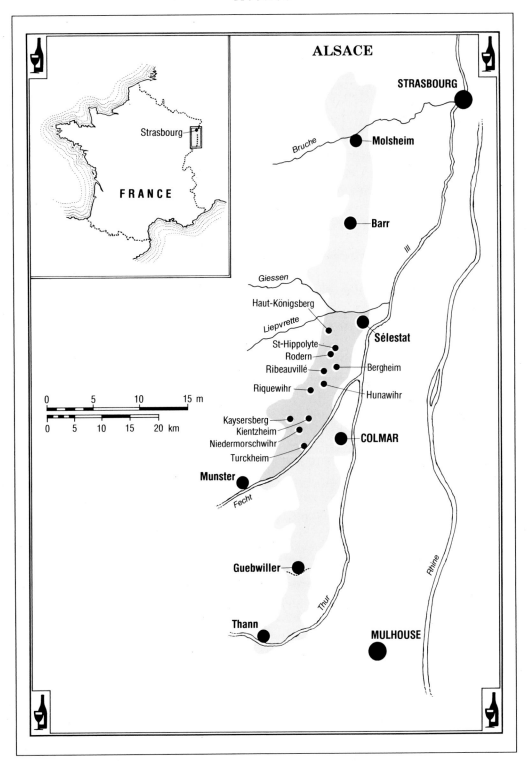

Grand Vin
Réserve Exceptionnelle } a class below *Grand Cru*, but their alcohol
Grand Réserve, etc. } content is above average.

Cuvée – the grower's own blend. It is the habit of smaller growers to make up their own blend and give it a name after *cuvée*. Each one has his own idea of proportions and ingredients, which ensures that you will be tasting something wholly original.

Edelzwicker – also a blend, of the better varieties.

Vendange Tardive – late harvest, literally.

Spätlese – the German term for late harvest. This means that the grapes were gathered after the general harvest and this gives an extra strength and sweetness to the resulting wines, the only ones which Alsace vinifies to be sweet. They will also be expensive because of extra work and risk involved.

There are two main departments in Alsace, the Haut Rhin and Bas Rhin, the south and north respectively, and the best wine regions are considered to be in the south. The Vosges mountains slope off towards the north thus leaving the wine-lands more exposed, whereas in the south they protect the land from rain and winds, allowing them to enjoy a particularly favourable climate. Colmar is regarded as the major wine capital, nearly all the villages around it are steeped in wine tradition and it is this part of Alsace which we have mapped out but, if you are exploring the upper half too, Barr and its immediate surrounds are the places to head for. Since Alsace is such an attractive and interesting place to visit, even if you are not drawn at all by its wine, it is well used to hordes of tourists and certainly could be said to be geared up and ready for the onslaught as the season approaches. Some towns and villages run the risk of being spoilt by over-commercialisation whilst others manage to wear it well; in general, if you become tired of coaches, crowds and souvenir shops, your best bet is to fan outwards and upwards towards the hills where there are still many delightful nooks and crannies to explore and photograph, but not quite so many cars and people. The wine is also best coming from these slopes, so you will benefit in both ways.

Prices are very reasonable for Alsace wines, with no vast differences between 'top' and 'bottom' quality as is often found in other more complicated areas. You have no need to choose from the lower prices for it is likely that these wines will be coming from the plains where quantity is the watchword, rather than from the chalky hillsides where all the quality wines are grown. A comparison between good local small growers' prices however, and those in the wine-shop windows, should tell you immediately where your personal choice is going to be made. Try to avoid buying in the most popular and heavily-visited towns, for apart from higher prices, the atmosphere is too highly charged with activity for you to enjoy a leisurely browse through what is offered.

Whilst on the subject of hills, mention must be made of the lovely *Route des Crêtes* running along the top of the Vosges, affording panoramic views on a clear day, with green signs denoting *fermes auberges* where you can join with other walkers, cyclists and tourists to enjoy good local food and drink. A maze of footpaths lies to either side of the route and hill tops are crowned with castle ruins. At the northern end of the route, the castle of Haut-Königsberg commands a magnificent view over St Hippolyte, the *route du vin* and the plains below, with Germany and the Rhine clearly visible on a good day. The castle can be visited and has regular opening hours.

Le Markstein, also along this route, allows the visitor to wander over a vast and well documented area of trenches, forts and dugouts from the First World War, which serve to remind us of Alsace's bitter history and its vulnerable position geographically.

Nearly all the prettiest and best preserved villages have a ban on through traffic which is a blessing, but it is a good idea to arrive as early as possible, for such is the historic interest of these beautiful buildings that it is not simply the European, American and Oriental tourists who flock there, there are numerous local school parties visiting too, as part of their education. If you blot out the 'extras' and let your mind wander back to what life must have been like here before tourism was invented, you can easily forget all about the wine you were going to find and simply lose yourself in cobbled streets where houses lean out to greet each other, gables almost touching, timbers form patterns against creamy washed walls and everywhere is bright with flowers, mostly geraniums, hanging down in baskets, tumbling out of pots on balconies or decorating already ornate fountains. Sparkling rivers run through many of the towns, crossed by narrow bridges, begging to be photographed, old houses bulging outwards along the banks as though at a push they would fall in. These buildings however are made of the finest stone, which could have something to do with the fact that so many survived the wars. Riquewihr in particular is a masterpiece, utterly typical of the district, and it came through those difficult years virtually unscathed.

Storks can still be spotted posing regally, often using the platforms and nests provided for them by local residents hoping for the good luck which they are supposed to bring. Here and there you can also see the beautifully coloured tiled roofs which are more familiar in Burgundy, and everywhere it seems there are huge barrels or ancient wine presses outside private homes, cafés and restaurants, never letting you really forget for a moment that the whole place is saturated in wine. The people of Alsace seem to me to reflect the sunshine and happy crowds; whether this is in my imagination or whether it really has something to do with the atmosphere of the region does not matter, it is there to see and hear. They speak amongst each other in an Alsatian dialect sounding rather like German, but will always change into French for visitors.

The language is yet another result of Alsace's history, for many people will speak German too, if you do, and several of their notices are also written in German. *Weinstub* and *weinprobe* signs in particular will be seen for denoting tasting facilities, and you cannot help but notice how many place names end in *heim* or *berg* for instance. Before I became reasonable at either language, I tended to mix up the two when in the area, not being sure which the locals preferred to use, and frequently began a sentence in French only to get stuck and finish it in German, finding to my amazement that I had been followed and they could do it too! A chance meeting at Turckheim wine fair with an old character of a grower sparked off a very heated discussion among the locals about which language should be taught as the more important one in the schools, everyone getting very hot under the collar about it; until then we had not really considered the question and it proved to us how you can only begin to get the feel of a new area by trying to communicate with local folk, asking them questions, and joining in events. The easiest and most natural way, for us at least, has always been through sharing an interest in the local wine, for there are very few people in the heart of the wine growing region of Alsace whose lives are not coloured by it or who do not depend on it to some degree.

Kientzheim has a wine museum, is central to the wine area, and provides that background knowledge which helps us to appreciate fully the work which goes on in the vineyard and the cellar in order to bring to us the distinctive wines of Alsace. Barr, Ribeauvillé and Colmar have colourful wine festivals in July and August, and on the first Sunday in September at Ribeauvillé, you can drink freely of wine from its fountain!

ADDRESS
Justin Boxler, 68230 Niedermorschwihr.
A family firm for 300 years, full range of wines including *Grand Cru*, tasting in the cellar. A generous, friendly grower whose family own the restaurant across the road.

LOCAL PRODUCTS AND SPECIALITIES
miel de sapin – a dark honey from bees up in the pinewoods of the Vosges
Munster cheese – it goes well with the local wine
Kougelhof – you can't miss this moulded fruit bread in the bakers' shops
Choucroute or *sauerkraut* made with Alsace wine has all manner of local sausages, bacon and hams added to it, each restaurateur adding 'extras' of his own design.

Quiches – cheesy tarts – the real thing, not our English copies!

Fruit tarts – Alsace specialises in symmetrically arranged fruits, grown locally, resting on a bed of creamy custard.

Fruit brandies – any fruit not sitting in tarts is distilled into potent and very expensive brandy. A tot of one of these at the end of a busy wine-trekking day could well be your final savouring of Alsace before retiring to dream of hills, vines and narrow, cobbled streets!

FURTHER INFORMATION
Association Départementale du Tourisme du Haut Rhin,
Hôtel de Département, 6800 COLMAR.

Sparkling rivers run through many of
the towns . . . Kaysersberg

The castle of Haut-Königsberg in the
foothills of the Vosges

BORDEAUX

On the banks of the wide Gironde lies Bordeaux, France's third largest port, but it is not the port that most of us think of when we hear the word, it conjures up instead a picture of the world's most famous fine wine, claret. To discover why the wine from Bordeaux is so important to the British it is necessary to look back into the history of the region beginning with the first century BC when *négociants*, or merchants, already existed before the vineyards themselves – wine was imported here by river before the Romans arrived to plant the first vines.

Not until the twelfth century, however, did the wine trade really flourish. The marriage of Eleanor of Aquitaine to Henry Plantagenet, future king of England brought about the popularity of claret, for among her other possessions were the wine-lands of Bordeaux. The English, typically, could not cope with the French word *clairet* used for the wine of those days and called it claret, which persists to this day, referring only to the red wines of course. Bordeaux' geographical position allowed the shipping of wine cheaply and easily to England in the Middle Ages whereas transport overland was then difficult. It was thus that the great love affair between the English and their claret began.

The Hundred Years War interrupted trade when Aquitaine became French again, but business then returned as usual and boomed until the French Revolution, by which time it had become fashionable to drink Bordeaux both in England and in France. Foreign merchants and shippers were attracted to the thriving port and the quarter of the *Quai des Chartrons*, still today the area occupied exclusively by shippers, came into being. Gladstone of England made some welcome tax changes in the late nineteenth century which facilitated the work of the London importers, who for many years had been practising *élevage*, bringing on the young imported wines in their own cellars and starting the vogue for selected vineyards in Bordeaux. Growers there were thus encouraged to improve and vie with each other and the famous 1855 Classification of the *crus* of the Médoc was a direct result of all this interest.

After the outbreak of phylloxera in the 1870's which almost destroyed the vineyards, and the economic repercussions following two World Wars, the story is again taken up by the great shipping families, whose forbears were those pioneers from the seventeenth and eighteenth centuries. They inter-married, châteaux changed hands, mergers were formed and so on, until in the 1970s prices went crazy, aided and abetted by unknowledgeable speculators, and the bottom fell out of the Bordeaux market.

Resulting from this, the great firms and shippers lost public confidence and the trend toward direct sales began, which is where you and I come in. The wines of Bordeaux are now more accessible than ever and rumours tell us that prices for the 'inaccessible' ones must soon tumble, so now is the time to go seeking. With the advent of technology available to all, many of the smaller growers are rapidly making wine of a standard excellent enough to make the well established firms take notice and the rapport between their price and quality is very attractive.

> *This wine is too good for toast drinking, my dear. You don't want to mix emotions up with a wine like that. You lose the taste.*
> HEMINGWAY

The Bordeaux vineyard occupies an area of land bigger than any other wine region in the world, offering a tremendous variety of wines, red, white, rosé and *mousseux*, not just the beloved claret, but since it is well organised and falls quite naturally into certain separate parts with separate characteristics to the wines, we shall look at each in turn, beginning with the Médoc.

MÉDOC

Old Médoc sayings refer to the fact that the vine likes its feet in the gravel and to be within sight of the river. It is not surprising therefore to find that all the best vineyards occupy a two-mile wide strip of land stretching up the peninsula north of Bordeaux overlooking the Gironde and growing in gravelly terrain, the small pebbles serving to drain the land and to retain the heat of the day long into the night so that the low growing vines can benefit from the extra warmth. The climate is not spectacular, but there are few extremes and the vines are often very old; all these factors, together with the inherited skills of the Bordelais growers are thought to combine to make the wines of the Médoc what they are.

GRAPE VARIETIES
Red: Cabernet Sauvignon, Cabernet Franc, Merlot, Malbec
White: Sauvignon, Sémillon, Muscadelle

These are the classic grape varieties used throughout Bordeaux, whose regional differences are accounted for in part by the proportions used in the vinification.

To help you orientate yourselves before setting out to explore the Médoc wines, it might help to look at the family tree below:

Bordeaux

Médoc

Haut-Médoc

Listrac	St-Estèphe	Pauillac	Margaux	St-Julien	Moulis

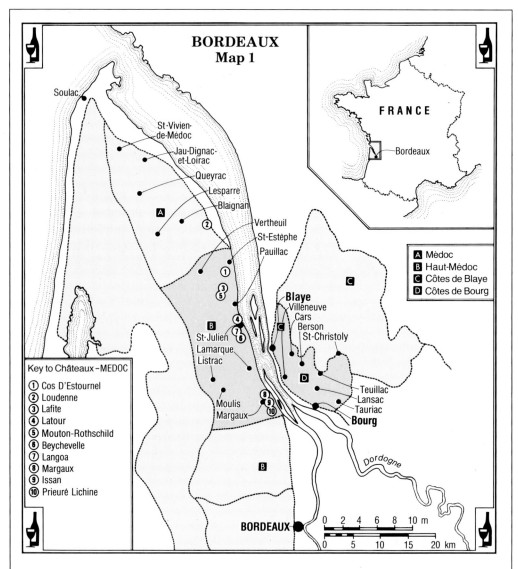

The rather dry information in an earlier chapter, 'Understanding Labels,' about appellations can now spring to life as you travel about and relate the individual ACs to their 'parent' ones, for the lower six are actually communes within the Haut-Médoc, the best part of the entire Médoc wine growing region, and they all come under the generic name of AC Bordeaux.

Numerous tourist circuits facilitate your excursions in the Médoc, but they are hardly necessary since you will be simply swept along from one glorious château to another, unless you turn up the side roads and begin your own circuit. There are plenty of opportunities for private buying, so select an area which is near to the long-established 'greats' and look for the kind of estate which most pleases you. The area named Bas-Médoc, lying north of Lesparre, represents fruitful territory for secret vineyards for here the hectic wine tourism begins to wane and one can feel more at ease in much more varied and interesting countryside. Verteuil on the way up to this region can easily waylay you with its Romanesque church and twelfth-century castle, now restored. The church has an arched door, particularly interesting to wine seekers for its sculpted figures show peasants tending the vines. The further north you explore, the nearer you come to the seaside resorts of this peninsula, further attractions for many people who like to combine their wine-drinking with other pursuits. Arcachon and its surrounding dunes, lakes and beaches are also popular places to combine with your Médoc wine tour.

One astute wine grower in the northern area, who enjoys meeting holiday makers up there, commented that the large châteaux are simply business concerns. They have a well-trained business manager at their head and everyone else is paid to help run the concern which continues automatically with nobody taking any personal interest in it. He added that the produce of many smaller châteaux around it is gathered up and used under the larger well-known name, thus adding to the anonymity of the product. If you have the opportunity, put his remark to the test, then compare that visit with one to a family firm, such as the two given below, and draw your own conclusions!

When buying wine from the Médoc, first decide whether you want to drink it fairly soon, or whether you are prepared to keep it and forget about it whilst it ages for some years in your cellar. The grower will probably have some which is vinified to be ready sooner than others, so consult him on this point.

Swept along from one glorious château to another . . . Cos d'Estournel, its builder had a penchant for the East!

ADDRESSES
Château Haut Bellevue, (Roses et fils), Lamarque.
For Haut-Médoc AC. A family concern, pride in traditional methods, no chemicals used. Homely, cheerful reception. Positioned between St-Julien and Margaux at the terminal of the Blaye-Lamarque ferry.

Château Haut-Gravat, (Alain Lanneau), 33 Jau-Dignac-Loirac.
For Médoc AC. Family property for three or four generations. All sales at the door, very handy for holiday-makers on beaches nearby. Ask for M. Lanneau rather than the château name when finding this one.

CHÂTEAUX

1 Cos d'Estournel – unusual pagoda style.
2 Loudenne – for its English connection.
3 Lafite
4 Latour } no comment!
5 Mouton-Rothschild
6 Beychevelle – for its beautiful gardens.
7 Langoa – beautiful eighteenth-century building.
8 Margaux – classical style.
9 Issan – fortified, with moat.
10 Prieuré Lichine – for its informative visit and friendly welcome, English spoken.

BOURG AND BLAYE

The ferry from Lamarque to Blaye links these two regions to the Médoc, being far more interesting than the bridge at Bordeaux, for apart from enjoying a leisurely view from the decks of both sides of the Gironde, you can get a closer look at some of the fishing boats and the intriguing contraptions erected at the Médoc side of the river. Fishing is very much in evidence in and around the Gironde and here on the banks of the river it is particularly interesting to see the numerous little jetties jutting out into the water using a pulley and net system.

In the fifteenth century, these two regions were far more famous than the mighty Médoc just across the water, in fact the Médoc was not mighty at all in those days, it was the poor relation! The part of both appellations which allows its vines to 'see the river' produces the best red wines of the region comparing very favourably with the *petits châteaux* of their illustrious neighbour, and further inland some excellent white is rapidly making a name for itself. Since Bourg and Blaye are relatively unknown to the wine-lover who enjoys a good Bordeaux red, their prices represent excellent value for money, so coupled with the fact that there is also good white wine and gently undulating pretty countryside to find it in, we would recommend your spending some time discovering the wines of these closely connected regions.

Blaye boasts the famous *citadelle* built in the seventeenth century to help stop smuggling and other dirty deeds from taking place. Much of it is still standing today, occupying a prime position on a rocky outcrop overlooking the whole of the estuary, a monument to Blaye's former important position with regard to the Bordeaux river trade. Bourg also has its attractions in the form of the Citadelle Château and its twin level situation whereby visitors can enjoy lovely views from the upper terraces over the lower-town roofs to the Gironde beyond. Not far away are the famous prehistoric caves of Pair-non-Pair, with their wall paintings of animals and fish.

The whole area affords the wine seeker easy hunting ground, for the little lanes leading from the villages on the pretty shore-line route twist and turn into vine country immediately with plenty of choice, since small private estates are scattered throughout the countryside. The pace of life around this district is noticeably relaxed compared with the bustle of the Médoc, and Bordeaux city in particular, and it is almost a relief to see other farming activities taking place in between concentrations of vineyard. An interesting tasting exercise might be to compare the two reds of Bourg and Blaye, for they are reputed to be quite different; the next obvious step is to compare them with the Médocs you've tried across the river – if you just love them all, don't worry about it, carry on tasting! Don't forget to discover the dry white Sauvignon wines of both regions, for we are reliably told that they are very much to the English taste and growers are planting more Sauvignon all the time to cater for the demand. Again, their price is most reasonable in view of their quality.

ADDRESSES
Château Crusquet de Lagarcie, (Philippe de Lagarcie),
Le Crusquet, Cars, 33390 Blaye.
For Blaye. Easily found on RN137. Interesting *chais*, huge barrels.

Château Moulin des Graves, (Jean Bost), Teuillac, 33710 Bourg.
For Bourg. Also on RN137. Run by son with help of parents. Among the first to plant white vines in Bourg. Friendly reception.

GRAVES

The wine district of Graves begins literally in the suburbs of Bordeaux itself and stretches southwards about sixty kilometres as far as Langon, encompassing the well-known Sauternes region and its neighbours at the southern end.

The name derives from what it sounds like, the gravelly land upon which the vines thrive which is similar to the Médoc, for the northern portion of the Graves is only, after all, an extension of the Médoc, with Bordeaux creeping outwards menacingly to the growers' concern, who witness their vineyards shrinking as the years go by. When the Médoc was still in its wild and dangerous state during the Middle Ages, the Graves wine, as its growers will be pleased to tell you, was going strong; in fact it was the red wine from the upper region which the English first grew to love, before the

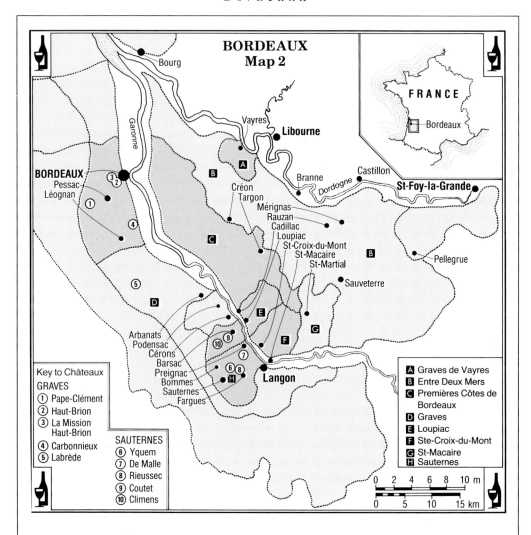

Key to Châteaux

GRAVES
① Pape-Clément
② Haut-Brion
③ La Mission Haut-Brion
④ Carbonnieux
⑤ Labrède

SAUTERNES
⑥ Yquem
⑦ De Malle
⑧ Rieussec
⑨ Coutet
⑩ Climens

Ⓐ Graves de Vayres
Ⓑ Entre Deux Mers
Ⓒ Premières Côtes de Bordeaux
Ⓓ Graves
Ⓔ Loupiac
Ⓕ Ste-Croix-du-Mont
Ⓖ St-Macaire
Ⓗ Sauternes

Médoc came into its own. Apart from the high quality red wine of the area nearest the city, Graves is known as a white wine area, although many places south of Léognan, the imaginary dividing line between upper and lower regions, will be found to produce both. It is a dry white, with a distinctive, pale yellow colour and a flavour all of its own which you might find difficult to choose words for, a wine quite different from the white Graves which I can remember having at Christmas time years ago.

The countryside south of Bordeaux is well wooded, making for pleasant wine-hunting forays and though the 'élite' end nearest Bordeaux possesses some great châteaux of legendary reputation, it is not overwhelmed with them as in the Haut-Médoc. A large area between these châteaux and Langon is wide open for exploration and plenty of bargains are to be found, for this area simply does not enjoy the reputation of its northern neighbours.

CHÂTEAUX
1   Pape-Clément – this Pope took the Papacy to Avignon in the early fourteenth century; his vineyard was one of Bordeaux' earliest.
2   Haut-Brion – for its long and colourful history.
3   La Mission-Haut-Brion.
4   Carbonnieux.
5   Labrède – the home of Montesquieu in beautiful grounds. This one is well worth a visit for its 'cultural' rather than its vinous aspect, and in its famous library during the May Bordeaux music festival, concerts are held.

ADDRESS
Château Lagrange, (Mme Y. Dozier), Arbanats.
Family property dating from the seventeenth century in a small area tipped as 'up and coming'. Makes a red and two whites. Very cordial welcome.

SAUTERNES AND BARSAC

Long life to the grape! for when summer is flown,
The age of our nectar shall gladden our own.

BYRON

Sauternes is world famous for its sweet white wines but, as with Champagne and Chablis for instance, it suffers from having its name 'pirated', often used without the final 's' to denote any wine which is very sweet. The real Sauternes can only be produced in five communes, Preignac, Bommes, Fargues, Barsac and Sauternes itself, and can be discovered by following the *Circuit du Sauternais*.

In the chapter entitled 'Wine and Country' an explanation of *pourriture noble* was given, which is precisely what the growers of Sauternes depend upon for their wine, but there are also a number of legends circulating regarding the initial discovery that wonderful wine could emerge from 'rotten' grapes. My favourite is the one from Germany: the Abbot of Schloss Johannisberg sent off his manservant one day to gain the necessary permission from the Bishop of Fulda to go ahead with harvesting his vineyard. The mission failed, the man did not return and the Abbot grew anxious for his crop, by then well-ripened. He kept faith with the local laws however and weeks later, after two more men had failed him, the sanction arrived. Too late alas, thought the Abbot sadly, look how much of the crop has now rotted. But he pressed those grapes separately just to see what would come of them and, lo and behold to everyone's astonishment, their greatest sweet wine ever resulted! This method reached Sauternes by some means or other and our first records of its results date from 1845.

The method of harvesting, the risks taken with the weather and the very small quantity of production all add up to the fact that Sauternes producers run a very costly business and it is this question of cost related to the quality of wine which is currently a sore point with consumers. Growers of other *liquoreux* wines in the vicinity, e.g. at Cérons and Ste-Croix-du-Mont speak of the returning vogue, particularly among young people for enjoying these wines as an apéritif. They will not however pay top Sauternes prices and it appears that as with the top Médoc wines, those of Sauternes are about to tumble.

CHÂTEAUX
  6   Yquem – the most prestigious, at Sauternes.
  7   de Malle – at Preignac, famous for its beauty.
  8   Rieussec – at Fargues.
  9   Climens }
 10   Coutet } – both in Barsac, which has its own AC.

ADDRESS
Domaine d'Arche-Pugneau, (Jean-Pierre Daney et fils),
Boutoc, Preignac 33210 Langon.
Situated right next to Yquem. Quality very fine but prices very reasonable.

CÉRONS

Cérons is the commune bordering Barsac to which you should go if you find that the Sauternes prices frighten you away, in spite of your love of that style of wine. Graves Supérieures, a *moelleux* white is also made in this district, the Cérons being said to lie somewhere between the two. Prices are most reasonable and such is the demand for the Cérons that our chosen château runs out of stock and has to disappoint clients occasionally. The new generation of growers is adding dynamism and recent technical knowledge to the tradition inherited with its properties and, all in all, we would say that in a few years' time when results become noticeable, this small area of *liquoreux* wines will be very much more in demand.

ADDRESS
Grand Enclos du Château de Cérons, (Olivier Lataste),
Place Charles de Gaulle, Cérons 33720 Podensac.
This château, part of the old Château de Cérons, produces a fine sweet wine, but also has Graves dry white and red. Helpful and friendly reception.

ENTRE-DEUX-MERS

Literally, this largest of all Bordeaux regions is 'between two rivers', the Garonne and the Dordogne, specialising in a dry white wine using the Sauvignon grape mainly, a wine which is very popular with English visitors and represents excellent value for money. The countryside is varied with lovely wooded areas as well as stretches of farm and pasture-land. Créon is considered the principal town of this pleasant region, and is an excellent example of a *bastide*. *Bastides* were built in the thirteenth and fourteenth centuries by the English and French rulers to mark out their respective territories. They are all built to a similar pattern of streets arranged on a square principal, with fortified walls and church, and a distinctively designed central square with arches and galleries surrounding it. Sauveterre de Guyenne is also a good example in this area. A circuit of abbeys is marked out in the Entre-deux-Mers which could well combine with your own wine circuit. Wine production is concentrated around the towns marked on the map, frequently involving small, family properties, where you will also find some very good red, marketed under the Bordeaux or Bordeaux Supérieur appellation.

ADDRESS
Château la Blanquerie, (Marcel Rougier),
Mérignas, 33350 Castillon-la-Bataille.
Family property, no chemicals used. Their reds are remarkable as well as the white. Friendly reception.

GRAVES DE VAYRES, STE-FOY-BORDEAUX, CÔTES DE BORDEAUX ST-MACAIRE

These three regions can be visited whilst exploring 'between the rivers,' all of them producing both red and white wine, but you will often find that they market their produce under the general appellation Bordeaux, for the local names mean so little to most people that it is a better commercial proposition. St-Macaire itself is interesting to explore for its medieval history and its old houses representing subsequent styles of architecture, and Ste-Foy-la-Grande was formerly a *bastide;* nowadays it is a lively town attracting visitors because of its pleasant position on the banks of the Dordogne, but many features of its past can be noticed if you take the time to stroll through its streets.

ADDRESS
Château Courtey, (Philippe Danies Sauvestre),
St-Martial, 33490 St-Macaire.
A serious young grower, his red sold under the Bordeaux and Bordeaux Supérieur label. Busy expanding the estate.

PREMIÈRES CÔTES DE BORDEAUX, CADILLAC, LOUPIAC, STE-CROIX-DU-MONT

The above regions represent a very interesting stretch of hunting ground since four distinctly different wine styles are to be found, all in the one strip of land bordering the right bank of the Garonne, and the area offers many other attractions to be combined with your tasting events. The Premières Côtes specialises in good red wines, particularly at its northern end, yet also makes a dry white and a sweet one, the latter being marketed under the name of Cadillac, its principal town. Cadillac would be a suitable base for forays in this region, for not only does it occupy a central position, but it is a fine example of a *bastide* and has the added interest of its seventeenth-century Château des Ducs d'Épernon. The château attracts visitors all the year round and offers interior as well as exterior tours.

Ste-Croix-du-Mont produces Sauternes-style wines at accessible prices and the quality can be very good indeed, as proved by the fact that at a recent professional blind tasting of about sixty good Sauternes wines, the bottle of Ste-Croix, naughtily slipped in by someone, came out in the top ten! In this area, one gets the impression that there is a strong feeling of 'us' and 'them', the former being the right bank producers of sweet wines and the latter being Sauternes; no-one suggests that right bank quality is equal to the top bottles of Sauternes, but it is inferred that the price differential is not justifiable.

Near to the château and church at Ste-Croix, there is a fascinating cave of oyster fossils to discover for those tourists pursuing ancient history as well as good wine, and certain vantage points around here give wonderful views across the river; Château d'Yquem is clearly visible.

ADDRESS
Château la Rame, (C. Arnaud et fils), Ste-Croix-du-Mont 33410 Cadillac.
Wonderful reception, with possibility of visit and meal in the tasting room whose windows offer the above mentioned panorama.

POMEROL

Pomerol, St-Émilion and Fronsac all cluster around Libourne, former *bastide* and port, which used to be a focal point for both river traffic and pilgrims passing through on their way to Compostela. Planted with vines since Roman times, they make red wines only.

Pomerol is only a tiny vineyard but is known the world over for its top quality and often fabulous prices, which makes it rather exclusive. The good news for secret château hunters is that if they seek hard enough in the right areas there are small growers using the same predominant grape, the Merlot, whose vineyards are situated on similar soil. However, it must be admitted that in this tightly packed area of vines it can be frustrating trying to find just the right place. Our advice is to look in Lalande-de-Pomerol and Néac, which border both Pomerol and St-Émilion. At both these spots, close to each other, there is still a good choice of venues but the prices are more affordable; at Lalande there is a beautifully preserved twelfth-century church with a fascinating history tying in with that of the region, making a wine visit doubly profitable.

ADDRESS
Château Bourseau, Lalande-de-Pomerol.
Near the church, pleasant reception. Owner has St-Émilion property also.

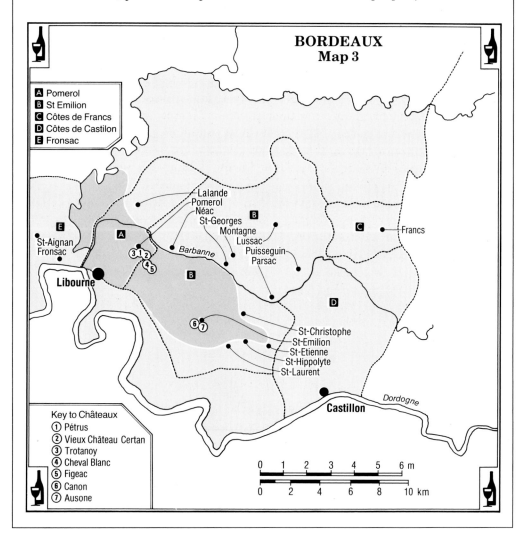

**BORDEAUX
Map 3**

A Pomerol
B St Emilion
C Côtes de Francs
D Côtes de Castilon
E Fronsac

Lalande
Pomerol
Néac
St-Georges
Montagne
Lussac
Puisseguin
Parsac

Francs

St-Aignan
Fronsac

Barbanne

Libourne

St-Christophe
St-Emilion
St-Etienne
St-Hippolyte
St-Laurent

Castillon
Dordogne

Key to Châteaux
① Pétrus
② Vieux Château Certan
③ Trotanoy
④ Cheval Blanc
⑤ Figeac
⑥ Canon
⑦ Ausone

0 1 2 3 4 5 6 m

0 2 4 6 8 10 km

CHÂTEAUX

1 Pétrus – the most expensive of Bordeaux wines.

2 Vieux Château Certan – one of the few good buildings of this area.

3 Trotanoy – has very old vines and an interesting origin, for its name relates to the French words for too much trouble *(trop d'ennuis)*, denoting how difficult it was to work the land. It is a fact that the clay noticeably present in Pomerol's soils and said to account for some of its wine's characteristics is not easy to handle in bad weather. A study of château names could well reveal a good deal about conditions and background history but we must leave this idea for someone else to pursue and move on to neighbouring St-Émilion.

ST-ÉMILION

One of the pilgrims to Compostela who didn't make it was St-Émilion, who on passing through the area was waylaid by 'a marvellous spring'. A spring of *what* we are not sure, for he went no further and his hermitage dwelling in the rocks can be visited today as you look around the picturesque town which grew up round him in the eighth century. Much of the town is medieval and is a welcome sight for those tourists who might be tired of the somewhat mundane districts of the Médoc for instance. It is however seething with activity in the summer season, so time your visit carefully to enjoy it to the full. St-Émilion's church, the thousand year old *église monolithe*, built in the rocks, is one of the town's chief attractions. It is here, in its cool depths, that the famous *Jurade* meet to decide whether they will give their seal of approval to the wine of the previous year's harvest – this ceremony dating back to the Middle Ages but still carrying weight today. With equal pomp and ceremony the red-robed brothers climb to the top of the Tour du Roi to proclaim that the harvest may begin and of course the wines of St-Émilion flow freely on both occasions.

St-Émilion wines are classified in a similar way to those across the river, having *Premier Grand Crus* and *Grand Crus*.

CHÂTEAUX

4 Cheval Blanc
5 Figeac } – Graves wines, grown on the gravelly plateau near to Pomerol.

6 Canon
7 Ausone } – Côtes wines, grown on the steep slopes near the town.

The amateur wine seeker can be easily overwhelmed by the sheer number of top quality, expensive châteaux, in which case we recommend you make for one of those five towns with St-Émilion added to their name and find somewhere small and friendly where the atmosphere is less highly charged. If you select carefully you can find places on the same terrain as Pomerol and St-Émilion's best wine, and need not be very far from either.

ADDRESS
Château Haut Milon, (Jean Boireau),
Les Jays, Les Artigues de Lussac, 33570 Lussac.
Warm reception. Position four kilometres from famous neighbours in Pomerol, on same soil. Family tradition but modern techniques, reasonable prices.

FRONSAC

The red wine of Fronsac is growing in popularity, with visible signs of expansion in the vineyards too in the shape of new plantings. It is an area of gentle beauty with little knolls featuring here and there, and its vineyards are tended immaculately, most of the vines being able to 'see the river' in true Bordeaux style. From a distance you can easily pick out the distinctive knoll which overlooks the town of Fronsac, crowned with the folly built there by the Duc de Richelieu in the eighteenth century. Charlemagne played a part in Fronsac's history too when he was busy subduing the Gascons there, in his insistence that wine should be transported in iron-circled barrels only. You will hear all about these things if you aim for that particular knoll, for it is there that our chosen venue is situated, and there is no extra charge for the wonderful panorama from the top or for the delightful way in which the elderly proprietor will tell you his stories. Fronsac's wine is strongly recommended if you like the Bordeaux style, but not the commerce or snob-value which often mars its discovery for many.

ADDRESS
Château de Fronsac, (P. Seurin),
33126 Fronsac.
Courteous welcome, tasting in underground rock cellar; views over Libourne, Pomerol, and St-Émilion for miles on a clear day.

CÔTES DE CASTILLON, CÔTES DE FRANCS

As Fronsac is Pomerol's neighbour, so are these two neighbours to St-Émilion, but are not considered to produce such good wines as Fronsac. It is nevertheless Bordeaux Supérieur standard and if you are in Castillon-la-Bataille, whose claim to fame is that it was there that the Hundred Years War came to an end, it would be worth sampling.

FURTHER INFORMATION
Comité Régional de Tourisme,
24, Allées de Tourney,
33000 Bordeaux.

St-Émilion from the church roof, Tour du Roi to the right

For information regarding visits to Bordeaux Châteaux write to:
Conseil Interprofessionel des Vins de Bordeaux,
Maison du Vin,
1, Cours du 30 Juillet, Bordeaux.

LOCAL PRODUCTS AND SPECIALITIES

The Gironde specialises in fish of almost every kind, from sardines and shrimps to sturgeon and lamprey.

Oysters *(huitres)* from the Arcachon basin come in all shapes and sizes and are often served with little spicy sausages.

Lamproie à la bordelaise is the name given to the local lamprey done in a sauce of the much loved shallots and of course red Bordeaux.

Cèpes are mushrooms local to Bordeaux; they feature in many dishes.

Some dishes are grilled *'aux sarments'* i.e. over vine prunings.

Macaroons are St-Émilion's sweet delicacy, and pralines belong to Blaye.

Foie gras is what the *liquoreux* producers would have us eat with their wine; can one afford both?

BURGUNDY

Burgundy's name, like that of Bordeaux, has been synonymous with fine wine for centuries, known all over the world, even by those who do not drink wine. As with Bordeaux, where the name simply means 'claret' to many people, Burgundy probably just means a 'heavy red wine' to many. Nothing could be further from the truth, as we hope to show in the following pages.

This wine should be eaten, it is too good to be drunk.

SWIFT

Although the two great names, Bordeaux and Burgundy would appear to be equally celebrated, their vineyards are totally unalike. Bordeaux boasts large residences and vast areas of vines owned by the one family or firm; in Burgundy there are very few such mansions and the vineyards are each owned and worked by a number of different growers, some having a small strip in each of several, dotted around the area. To discover the reason for this fragmentation of land ownership, we must look into Burgundy's history, starting in the sixth century when it was a kingdom. The king gave away one of his vineyards to the local monastic order; the monks were naturally delighted and with typical zeal developed the land. The king's example was then followed by the noblemen who subsequently ruled Burgundy when it became a duchy, with the result that over the centuries much of what we know today as the 'expensive area' was owned and managed by the religious orders. Bernard of Clairvaux inspired his monks to work harder at producing the wine instead of drinking it, until it was not long before many of the finest vineyards came into being, remaining exclusive to this day.

The French Revolution however, during its bloody period of aggressive anti-Church and anti-Establishment activity, ensured that the vinelands were taken from the Church and sold off to the people in small parcels, thus creating the system of multi-ownership which exists today. Clos de Vougeot for example is owned by more than a hundred people! The advantage of this system is that the grower does not have all his eggs in one basket when there are disasters such as hail or frost, but the disadvantage is that the customer can easily become confused by the appellation system, for here in Burgundy, many individual plots or *climats* can have their own appellation.

For our purposes in this book, the Burgundy vineyard will be divided into five major regions, starting with the most northern one and moving south.

CHABLIS

First of all, let us state clearly that there is only one Chablis. As in the case of Sauternes and Champagne, there are many 'copyists' who use the name on their label, the better to sell the wine, which at best might be something similar, but has no legal right whatever to use the name.

The history of Chablis is interesting, for it explains why there is such a large gap between its small vineyard and the Côte d'Or, starting just south of Dijon. The vineyard of Chablis once accounted for two-thirds of Burgundy's output and covered the area which now rather isolates it from the rest. The Cistercian monks from nearby Pontigny Abbey worked their magic spell on the land, having gained their practical knowledge in the Côte d'Or region and, from the twelfth century until the late nineteenth, the vineyard enjoyed great prestige. Then came phylloxera (see p.23), which effectively wiped out most of Chablis. Work in this northern vineyard, where frosts can annihilate half a crop in one or two nights, where much of the land has to rest for long periods, and where the terrain is difficult to handle, had always been an unequal struggle and many growers found phylloxera to be the last straw and gave up. Only the parts around Chablis town were replanted after the disaster, hence the vineyard's position today, but in the 1960s and '70s, heaters and sprinkler systems came into use against frosts, growers took heart again and began replanting at a tremendous pace. Demand for Chablis is high, many new areas are being created and the story goes on. . . .

Chablis wine has its own hierarchy, Grand Cru, Premier Cru, Chablis and Petit Chablis, the differences in character accounted for basically by the terrain on which the vines are grown, and their exposure to the sun. All the wine is dry and white, with what the experts will call a 'flinty' taste – see what word you can dream up! It is a wine to be drunk young and fresh, particularly the Chablis and Petit Chablis, and can be found easily enough in all the little villages surrounding the town. Avoid buying in the town shops themselves, simply use their windows to gain an idea of price in relationship to the four levels, but do go into the wine information bureau, for this way you can absorb more background knowledge and find a wine route to follow.

THE GRAND CRU VINEYARDS
They are all close together within a stone's throw of the town, but across the river:

1	Les Clos	3	Blanchots	5	Grenouilles	7	Bougros
2	Les Preuses	4	Valmur	6	Vaudésir		

Premier Cru vineyards surround these, with others at the Chablis side of the Serein, but you will find that the venue you choose could have holdings dotted about everywhere; the notice-board can be of some help however, for it usually announces which wines are for sale. Tour the villages therefore, and simply stop where the reception looks friendly and the price suits your pocket. Of particular interest when you travel through the vineyards, especially the better ones, are the 'bougies', in their various forms, and the sprinkler systems, essential equipment for countering spring frosts. The *bougies*, literally 'candles', keep the air circulating and the sprinkler system works on the principle of the igloo, where residual heat is trapped inside the ice formed after water has frozen on the plants when a frost occurs.

ADDRESSES
Domaine Jean-Claude Dauvissat, 2 et 10 Grande-Rue, Beines 8900 Chablis.
For Chablis and Premier Cru; a generous friendly welcome in pleasant tasting area. Lots of modern equipment to see, if you are interested.

Roland Lavantureux, Lignorelles (Yonne).
For Chablis and Petit Chablis. A smaller firm, very friendly, family welcome.

It must not be forgotten that there was once a much bigger vineyard around Auxerre, whose remnants can now be explored by taking the little roads through its wine villages. Irancy, Chitry, Courgis, St Bris le Vineux, and Coulanges la Vineuse offer a delightful detour in the Chablis vicinity, where the countryside is particularly lovely in spring when the cherry trees are in blossom. Here too they do their own thing with the Sauvignon, as opposed to the usual Burgundy grapes, to produce Burgundy's only VDQS wine, Sauvignon de St Bris. At Irancy you might be able to add another grape variety to your repertoire before it dies out, the César.

GRAPE VARIETIES
Pinot Noir – for best reds
Gamay – for secondary reds, but particularly right for Beaujolais
Chardonnay – for best whites
Aligoté – a secondary white, particularly good in St-Aubin/Bouzeron area
Pinot Noir/Gamay – together these two make Passe-Tout-Grains, pleasant to drink in situ

These are the classical grape varieties used throughout all the regions of Burgundy, whose generic appellation is *bourgogne*.

CÔTE DE NUITS, CÔTE D'OR

The Côte de Nuits is the name given to the northern half of this very famous and valuable stretch of land which begins just south of Dijon. Following the *route des grands crus*, it soon becomes apparent that you are winding through one gold mine of vines after another, if you are at all familiar with the world's most highly priced labels. Why are these wines so highly priced, the wine novice might well ask. The answer lies in the scarcity factor. Because some of these *climats* are so small, and their quality so keenly sought after by connoisseurs, the laws of supply and demand tell us the rest. However, such is the distinctive nature of these small plots that the neighbour of a famous and expensive one could quite easily be producing mediocre wine at inflated prices, creating an obvious difficulty for the wine-seeker who would like something of good value from the area but cannot or will not afford the greatest.

We would recommend that you admire the 'greats' from a distance and head into the *arrière-pays*, or back roads, nearby to taste and purchase, for our travels this year have revealed a source which perfectly fits the description of secret vineyard. But first, in the absence of châteaux, a few of the most famous vineyards:

FAMOUS VINEYARDS
1 La Romanée-Conti, Grand Cru, at Vosne-Romanée
2 Clos de Vougeot, Grand Cru, at Vougeot
3 Chambertin, Grand Cru, at Gevrey-Chambertin
4 Grands-Échézeaux, Grand Cru, at Flagey
5 Les Musigny, Grand Cru, at Chambolle-Musigny
6 Les St-Georges, Premier Cru, at Nuits-St-Georges

A visit to the château of Clos de Vougeot would allow you to appreciate its part in Burgundy's history, for inside can be seen the enormous presses from the twelfth century when the Cistercian monks first worked this famous piece of land. Today the *Chevaliers du Tastevin* (see p.37) own the château and there in the Grand Cellier their dinners and other celebrations take place, all in the cause of promoting the good name of Burgundy they will have us believe.

Back now to our new-found source of Burgundy wine. The *Circuit des Hautes Côtes* takes you through landscape well described by one leaflet as 'having more humps than an army of camels', past poverty-stricken looking stone cottages, heaped together in an enchanting new world compared with the tourist plains below and their traffic. There are sixteen wine communes to choose from, all reached by descending a little from the circuit, and exciting things are happening here regarding expansion of the vineyards and quality of the wines. Suffice it to say that quality is already rivalling Premier Cru standards of major firms which at first were sceptical and now are slightly worried about the Hautes Côtes' rapid rise to fame. Here are secret vineyards *par excellence* – no-one could suspect their existence who had not been told about them. Visit La Maison des Hautes Côtes at Marey lès Fussey for information and an excellent Burgundian meal at very modest prices.

ADDRESS
Domain Montmain, (Bernard Hudelot), Villars Fontaine.
President of the Maison, M. Hudelot makes wine which now saves us the need of looking elsewhere in the Côte de Nuits. There are plans for *gîtes* near his beautifully situated premises.

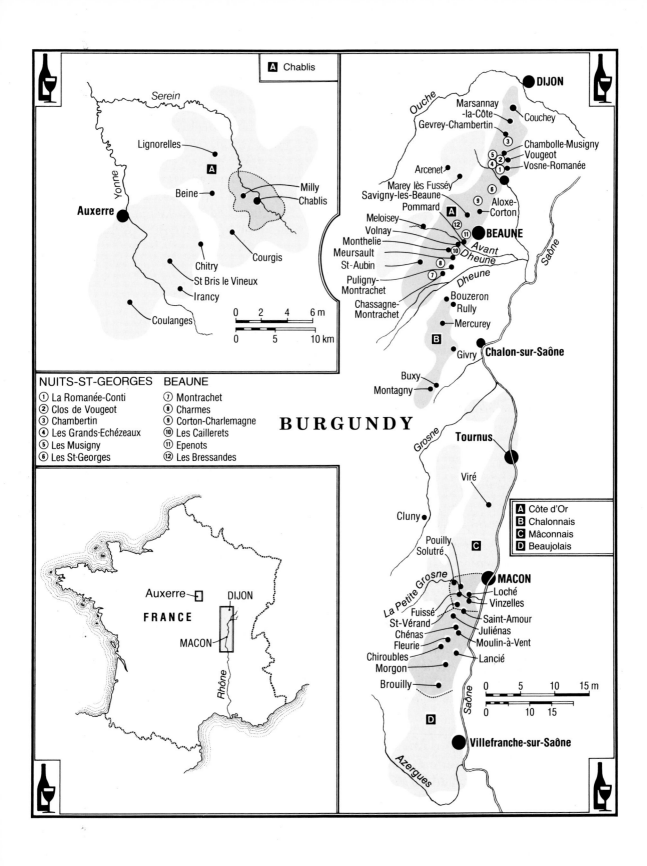

A Chablis

Serein

Lignorelles

A

Beine

Milly
Chablis

Yonne

Auxerre

Chitry
St Bris le Vineux
Irancy

Courgis

Coulanges

0   2   4   6 m

0   5   10 km

DIJON

Ouche

Marsannay
-la-Côte
Gevrey-Chambertin

Couchey

Chambolle-Musigny
⑤ ② Vougeot
④ ⑩ Vosne-Romanée
①

Arcenet

⑥

Marey lès Fusséy
Savigny-les-Beaune
Pommard

⑨

Aloxe-
Corton

A

Meloisey
Volnay
Monthelie
Meursault
St-Aubin
Puligny-
Montrachet

⑫
⑪ **BEAUNE**
⑩ *Avant*
Dheune
⑧
⑦ *Dheune*

Chassagne-
Montrachet

Bouzeron
Rully

Mercurey

B

Givry

Chalon-sur-Saône

Buxy

Montagny

B U R G U N D Y

Grosne

Tournus

Viré

NUITS-ST-GEORGES

① La Romanée-Conti
② Clos de Vougeot
③ Chambertin
④ Les Grands-Echézeaux
⑤ Les Musigny
⑥ Les St-Georges

BEAUNE

⑦ Montrachet
⑧ Charmes
⑨ Corton-Charlemagne
⑩ Les Caillerets
⑪ Epenots
⑫ Les Bressandes

Cluny

Pouilly
Solutré

C

A Côte d'Or
B Chalonnais
C Mâconnais
D Beaujolais

La Petite Grosne

Loché
Vinzelles

Fuissé

Saint-Amour

St-Vérand
Chénas
Fleurie

Chiroubles
Morgon

Brouilly

MACON

Juliénas
Moulin-à-Vent

Lancié

Grosne

Auxerre

DIJON

FRANCE

MACON

Rhône

Saône

0   5   10   15 m

0   10   15

D

Azergues

Villefranche-sur-Saône

The Hautes Côtes vinelands grow fruits as well as the vine, deriving considerable income from their use in the making of liqueurs, particularly around Nuits-St-Georges. A visit to a *liquoriste* complements a wine tour very nicely, for the two liquids together in the correct proportion give the aperitif, kir, when it is a question of blackcurrant liqueur at least. That is the most popular variety but a visit to the address below will show you how many fruits are used and how potent the brew can be! M. Joannet was keen to tell us that one of his raspberry plants was from England, the Lloyd George, but his pronunciation was so French that it took us ten minutes to absorb this fact – so now you know if the subject crops up when you make a visit.

ADDRESS
Jean Baptiste Joannet, Arcenant, 21700 Nuits-St-Georges.

CÔTE DE BEAUNE, CÔTE D'OR

The Côte de Beaune, the southern half of the Côte d'Or, is a wider area than that of its neighbour and is famous for both red and dry white wine. Many of its wines have achieved world renown, but happily there are plenty of more humble ones of high quality within reach of most of us. In general, the Nuits are deeper in colour and longer living compared with the Beaunes, which do not need to be kept for so long before being enjoyed. The white wines, many of them world famous, tend to be grouped together south of Mersault.

FAMOUS VINEYARDS
  7   Montrachet, white Grand Cru, at Chassagne and Puligny-Montrachet
  8   Charmes, white Premier Cru, at Mersault
  9   Corton-Charlemagne, white Grand Cru at Aloxe-Corton
 10   Les Caillerets, red Premier Cru, at Volnay
 11   Épenots, red Premier Cru, at Pommard
 12   Les Bressandes, red Premier Cru, at Beaune

Again, a *route des grands crus* takes us past all these and many other notorious places, and there is Beaune itself to visit, which without doubt is the trading centre of all Burgundy's wine. The streets are almost awash with wine but the visitor will do well to keep his tasting and buying to the villages themselves and just enjoy the atmosphere of a busy wine capital for an hour or so. A visit to the Hôtel Dieu belonging to the Hospices de Beaune is a must, if only to see its multi-coloured tiled roof, typical but finer than all the others of the area. Built in the fifteenth century, it is a charity hospital and makes much of its income from the proceeds of the Annual November Auction which sells its wines from vineyards donated by generous Burgundian growers. Much prestige is attached to the ownership of some Hospices de Beaune, buyers being attracted from all over the world.

However, all this is a little high-powered and we recommend you take the Hautes Côtes de Beaune route away into the nearby hills and do your tasting in a more peaceful and leisurely atmosphere where the scenery is even more lovely than that of the Nuits route, with panoramas, little villages of Roman interest, clusters of ancient farm buildings and plenty of good wine. These growers are represented too at the Maison des Hautes Côtes mentioned in the previous section. Not far from this area is the well visited La Rochepot castle, perched on a knoll but surrounded by woods, making photography difficult. It has been completely restored and is particularly attractive for its many towers of coloured tiles.

Several villages in this area of Beaune wine are placed in strategic positions sharing soil and conditions with famous neighbours, but not pricing their wines accordingly, where wine hunting can be quite profitable. One of these is St-Aubin, sitting among Premier Cru lands, but with a little detective work, you will find others – it's great fun, for we all love to think we have found a bargain.

ADDRESS
Jean Lafouge, St-Aubin 21190 Mersault.
Next to the tenth-century church. St-Aubin, Côte de Beaune and other wines on sale. Typical friendly Burgundian and wife. Neighbour of many 'greats'.

One word of advice we would offer to those who want to buy from one of the celebrated firms in the Côte d'Or is to ask about the keeping qualities of your preferred wine. There is no point in keeping a wine simply to say you've got one in the cellar, but it would also be a shame to open it before it had reached its peak, especially if it was expensive. Remember too, to read the labels carefully, for if you think you have got something dirt cheap, its likely that you have missed some vital remarks in the description!

THE CHALONNAIS

The Chalonnais vineyard used to be far more abundant, being at one time highly favoured by the gentry, but now its wines seem to be rather in the shadow of neighbouring Beaune. We would call it good hunting ground therefore, realising that there is excellent wine to be found, but as always when eclipsed by something more renowned, the prices are modest. There is also variety to attract wine-seekers, both in wine-styles and the countryside which demonstrates that people actually do other things here apart from growing vines.

ALIGOTÉ BOUZERON

The first discovery to be made when travelling south is the Aligoté wine of Bouzeron, just outside Chagny. This small area is particularly suited to the Aligoté grape, rather

The peaceful countryside of Chalonnais makes touring a pleasure . . . the Château de Sercy, near Buxy

looked down on in the 'high class' regions. Here it is beautifully refreshing, a wine to be drunk young, or to be combined with cassis liqueur to make the popular aperitif, kir.

ADDRESS
R. et J. Bonnet, Bouzeron 71150 Chagny.
Next to the church. Very friendly family reception.

The peaceful Chalonnais countryside makes touring a pleasure; here there is no pressure exerted on you to gaze at vast vineyards, you take in other delights and simply make a wine stop when the time and place seem right. A condensed guide to the four appellations will help focus your tour.

Rully – Reds and whites and a sparkling one, *crémant*, to try for the fun of it. Very pretty village in the hills.

Mercurey – The 'capital' of the area; mostly red wines comparing favourably with Beaune's. Vast choice of venue.

Givry – Mostly red wines. Historic town.

Montagny – Entirely white wine. Town noted for the longevity of its inhabitants. Could it be due to its wines?

All these areas are composed of more than the one commune, so it is not essential to visit that particular place, you can fan out into the little villages.

ADDRESS
Domaine Jean Vachet, (M. Jean Vachet), St-Vallerin, 71390 Buxy.
For a variety of prize-winning Chalon wines, including a Premier Cru. Helpful
reception.

THE MÂCONNAIS

To happy converts bosomed deep in vines
Where slumber abbots, purple as their wines.

POPE

Mâcon's present fame tends to rely heavily on the Pouilly-Fuissé wine which has only recently become very much in demand, but its history tells us that the monks of nearby Cluny were busily tending the vines long ago and teaching the simple folk how to improve their techniques. Burgundy wines would not be the quality they are today if it had not been for the powerful religious orders of those days and their particular skills and knowledge of viticulture. (I find it tempting to picture what wonderful occasions their services must have been in some of the fine wine districts, and how difficult it must have been to concentrate on the business in hand after a full day's devotions involving the fruits of the vine.) Cluny itself is easily reached when visiting the Mâconnais and of course a few lines here cannot hope to do justice to what lies behind its name, for from the Middle Ages right up to the Revolution it has had a remarkable influence on not only religious life, but also on the arts, politics and philosophy. A visit inside will take time as there are generally crowds of tourists but plenty can be seen or guessed at by a walk around the town.

Louis XIV is also involved in the story of Mâcon, for thanks to the heroic efforts of one Monsieur Brosse, who managed to reach Paris after a hazardous journey with a couple of barrels on a cart, the king discovered its qualities and thus made famous the name of Mâcon by filling the royal cellars with it.

Much of the ordinary Mâcon wine is marketed by the co-operatives since there are so many small growers scattered about, but their product is usually very good and is reasonably priced for everyday use. Both red and white are made, though the reds seem to be rather eclipsed by the abundance of Beaujolais so near in the south. Mâcon-Villages is the better white, having the commune's name attached to it, but it is the wine of Pouilly-Fuissé which attracts the attention here.

POUILLY-FUISSÉ

Rummaging around the four communes producing this wine can be great fun, for they all seem to be reached by numerous little lanes leading deep into the countryside with the same signposts cropping up whichever way you turn. We eventually homed in on our venue through keeping the two enormous stark outcrops of rock in the position we thought they should be; certainly you cannot fail to see the rock of

Vergisson and the rock of Solutré. The prehistoric finds below the rock of Solutré are world famous, this place having given its name to the era of 15,000–12,000BC, the Solutrean period. It is assumed by archeologists that primitive hunters drove their prey to the edge of the rock, then frightened it into jumping off in confusion, for it is mainly the remains of horses which have been found. Skeletons of men have also been discovered, and those interested in looking into the whole story revealed by this area will find the museum at Mâcon the best place to go.

Owing to its fashionable popularity perhaps, Pouilly-Fuissé has become quite highly priced, a factor which is leading some of its adherents to find something very similar but more reasonable, Pouilly-Loché and Pouilly-Vinzelles, which have their own appellations. A more recent appellation, St-Véran, is also attracting buyers, for it is produced at the foot of the two great rocks on the same type of terrain as the Pouilly-Fuissé.

People like to talk of '*un goût de terroir*' when discussing the taste of Pouilly-Fuissé wine, literally a taste of the soil, something to do with the limestone and slate on which it is grown no doubt; also much vaunted is its greenish tinge when very young, which is the ideal time to enjoy the wine, for although some can keep for more than five years, they do not improve in quality and even risk losing their perfume.

ADDRESSES
André Forest, Vergisson 71960 Pierreclos.
For Pouilly-Fuissé. Pleasant reception, very helpful.

Domaine des Deux Roches, Davayé, 71960 Pierreclos.
For St-Véran. Friendly *vigneron*, long-established family concern.

BEAUJOLAIS

> *Pour out the wine without restrain or stay,*
> *Pour not by cups but by the belly-full,*
> *Pour out to all that wull.*
>
> SWIFT

It hardly seems necessary to give the Beaujolais an introduction, so popular has it become all over the world, particularly during the last decade. The rolling country is covered in vineyards as far as the eye can see, and if you look from the foothills of the Monts de Beaujolais, that's a very long way, for these hills such as the Mont de Brouilly give the visitor a beautiful view over the whole region, beyond the Saône plains even. There is no need of a notice to announce the Beaujolais vineyard as you arrive from the Mâcon direction, for the stubby Gamay vines are immediately noticeable after their more stately, highly-pruned Chardonnay neighbours. Here on granite-based soil the Gamay shows what it can do given the right conditions, and the result is a luscious, fruity, aromatic, red wine which needs no 'education' of the palate.

The region divides quite neatly into an upper and lower part, Haut and Bas, the better quality wine being produced in the northern upper section, which actually overlaps the Mâconnais at St-Amour. Four distinct qualities of wine are made, each with its own AC:

Beaujolais – Much of it comes from the Bas Beaujolais.

Beaujolais Supérieur – Having a slightly higher alcohol content.

Beaujolais-Villages – Thirty-seven villages possess the right to use this AC to gain which they must conform to stricter rules of production and pruning.

Nine Crus – These nine villages are considered to produce wine of outstanding, recognisable qualities.

THE CRUS

Moulin à Vent – known as the best.

Fleurie – rival of Moulin à Vent.

Juliénas ⎫
Morgon ⎭ – these two can age longer than most.

St-Amour – find here also Beaujolais blanc, to compare with Pouilly-Fuissé.

Chiroubles – one for early drinking, within a few months.

Côte de Brouilly ⎫
Brouilly ⎭ – can *you* tell the difference?

Beaujolais *nouveau*, or *primeur* as it is more often called in France, has all disappeared by December, so don't expect to find any on your summer holidays! November 15th is the great day each year when the new wine is released. It has become the fashion to acquire some as soon as possible after that date in most countries; teams of cars race there, lorries line the streets waiting their turn to be loaded, and restaurateurs spend a fortune on what used to be such a simple pleasure, quaffed in large glasses in nearby Lyon, by people who class it as their third river after the Rhône and Saône. Let's hope that big business will not spoil the happy atmosphere of this very attractive countryside and that growers will not concentrate too hard on vinifying their *crus* to be long living wines, for the essence of Beaujolais is surely its youthful freshness.

The Beaujolais method of carbonic maceration accounts for this appealing aspect of fruitiness and flowery aroma and is now being copied to a certain extent in other regions in order to please the public who tend to like wines which are ready *now* rather than in five or ten years' time.

There is no need to point out specific hunting grounds in this district, except to say that there really is no call in our opinion to seek out the top *crus*, neither is there any need to buy from the lowest price range, for the quality will not be anything like that of the Beaujolais-Villages which are all reasonably priced and readily available. Communes which are making wine of this latter category always advertise the fact in

The Beaujolais, one of France's uncomplicated areas of wine, designed for pure enjoyment – Fleurie here

range, Beaujolais *simple*, his *village*, and a *cru*, then you can taste them all and discover the differences. In the Beaujolais there's plenty of space for everyone and plenty of choice of venue; we consider it one of France's uncomplicated areas of wine, designed for pure enjoyment.

ADDRESSES
Domaine du Penlois, (M. Besson), Lancié.
Offers *simple*, Lancié and Morgon, one of the *crus*. Friendly venue.

Les Chaffrangeons, (Robert Depardon), Fleurie 69.
Offers Fleurie only and a very friendly welcome in an interesting tasting room.

If you are heading southwards out of the Beaujolais, you will soon find yourself in Pierres Dorées countryside, whose name is derived from the warmly golden-coloured stone quarried locally. Pretty little rural villages made almost entirely of this are scattered throughout the area, where the vineyards are less in evidence, being interspersed among farmland.

ST VINCENT
St Vincent is the patron saint of the wine-growers of France and appears to be especially loved by the people of Burgundy, who celebrate with a holiday in many wine districts on January 22nd. His statue can be found, however, not in Burgundy, but in Bordeaux (where he was turned to stone for his misdemeanours) and on view in

the cellars of La Mission-Haut-Brion where he met his downfall. What did he do to deserve such punishment? He apparently experienced a great yearning for the wines of his native land when in Heaven, and was granted permission to go back down and indulge for a while, but alas, the famous reds of Graves delayed him and cost him his loftier position for ever.

LOCAL PRODUCTS AND SPECIALITIES

Burgundy is known for its gastronomy and in an area as extended as our wine region, it would be difficult to choose just a few representative dishes. However. . .

Boeuf Bourgignon – local Charolais beef, stewed in wine. How many of us at home use *real* Burgundy?

Poulet de Bresse – a society actually exists to protect the name and reputation of these succulent chickens.

Snails, the *gros bourgogne* variety, apparently feed on the vine leaves. Does this add to their quality one wonders?

Fish, with *meurette* sauce made with wine.

Coq au vin – its nothing like ours!

Dijon mustard, *cassis* liqueur and spiced bread.

Let it be known that the Burgundians like their food and don't mind admitting it – why not join them?

FURTHER INFORMATION
Comité Régional de Tourisme,
Conseil Régional, BP1602, 21035 Dijon Cedex.

Follow the *route des Pierres Dorées*, to explore these villages built of golden stone

CHAMPAGNE

The majority of us think of Champagne as the best known of all sparkling wines, whose chief use is to help us celebrate any grand occasion such as weddings, twenty-firsts and christenings. It is associated with excess too, and waste; the rich and famous hold lavish parties where it is poured over people's heads for a joke, squirted at friends, even showered under. Why has it achieved such a reputation, why is it so highly priced, and is there anything else to drink in Champagne other than Champagne? Let's look at some of the answers to set the scene for a wine tour through this area not far from Paris.

The connection between Champagne drinking and high living goes right back to its earliest history in France when in the eighteenth century it became fashionable for the aristocracy to accompany all their activities of dubious moral character with the drinking of this new and unusual-style wine. The first 'reps' from the famous Houses of Champagne, whose names still flourish, must have done a fantastic job, well worthy of promotion, for the craze spread rapidly from Paris throughout the capitals of the world. The wine's reputation lives on as firmly today as ever. Even in those early days the wine was a luxury for no-one had then mastered the way to stop the bottles from exploding under pressure, with the result that much was lost and the wine was scarce and expensive; such was the historical foundation for the 'snob' value of Champagne, some of which still lingers in Britain.

The answer to the second question, why is it so highly priced, even today when technology has eliminated nearly all explosions save those of the cork, lies in the *champenois* method of wine-making and the fact that it has to be stored for at least a year, and often up to five, before being sold. It is an expensive business for the maker. A guided tour of a Champagne cellar is strongly recommended so that you can appreciate for yourself exactly what goes into your bottle, but we propose to outline very simply the various processes, since they differ from those general ones discussed in chapter two.

MAKING CHAMPAGNE

Harvesting and pressing: with infinite care taken to ensure that the grapes are not damaged at all, they are quickly taken to the nearest *vendangeoire* or pressing house. Speed and care are essential lest any colour from the skin of the black grapes used should be transferred. Wine is vinified as for classical white.

Blending: Champagne is traditionally a blend of different years' produce, unless it is to be a vintage one when it is the produce of that one year only. The blends of all the large Houses will vary, according to their own preference, but will remain consistent within the House itself.

Champagnisation: in Spring, sugar and yeasts are added, the wine is bottled and secondary fermentation begins, i.e. bubbles are formed. During this period the wine lies on its side in a cool cellar for a minimum of one year.

Remuage and **dégorgement:** sediment is formed by now. For a period of two or three months the bottles are moved gradually and systematically *(remuage)*, until they have gathered the sediment in the neck, being placed in special racks *(pupitres)*, then the sediment is removed *(dégorgement)* by freezing the necks, uncorking and shooting out that small portion.

Dosage: the bottle is topped up with wine from the same blend and an addition of sugar according to requirement.

This very simplified description of the Champagne process will hopefully begin to answer why it is so expensive, but an informative tour through a cellar brings it to life; below we recommend an excellent address where you can take a tour and will not be hemmed in by scores of other people or overwhelmed by commercialisation.

The question of whether there are any other wines to seek out in Champagne, can be answered in the affirmative for there are red and white still wines given the name Coteaux Champenois, and a rather exclusive rosé from one small area of the Aube region, le rosé des Riceys. The best reds are reputed to be around Bouzy and the best whites are south of the Marne in the Blanc de Blancs stretch of vineyard.

ADDRESS
Morel, père et fils, 93, Rue Général de Gaulle, 10340 Les Riceys.
Specialises in the unusual rosé, which is not cheap incidentally. Champagne is also made.

Since Champagne will probably be your chief interest, some guidance may be helpful for finding your own producer, for it would appear on first looking through the region that everyone is offering it, from the smallest village grower to the world famous Champagne House. How to choose must be a question which arises instantly when confronted with such a situation, particularly since this wine is more expensive than many others and you need to feel sure of receiving good value for money.

The Champagne production tends to concentrate in four main areas, the Montagne de Reims, the valley of the Marne, the Blanc de Blancs, and the Aube region, separated from these by about one hundred kilometres of farmland. The 'capitals' of Champagne are Reims and Épernay, Reims being of course a cathedral city of great interest to tourists, and both of them seething with Champagne activity making it very hard for the visitor to know where to go for the type of visit he has in mind. To solve the problem, we would recommend a tour around the very attractive Aube region, following its wine route signs from one point of interest to another. You will thus get the feel of Champagne before venturing into the more heavily commercialised areas where people flock annually.

Les Riceys commune is a particularly interesting and picturesque cluster of villages, a good spot for making your base for a visit. Further north a visit to the famous Cristalleries Royales de Champagne at Bayel, where you can tour the glass-making factory might tempt you to buy a few glasses of the right design for your souvenir wine of the region.

THE AUBE

The story of this region of Champagne is poignant. In the post-phylloxera period the area of vineyard was drastically cut by half and the *vignerons*, who already had a difficult task on their tiny parcels of land, were further hit by the awful harvest and bitter winter of 1910. Added to this was the fact that the Midi wines were starting to flood into the rest of France with the advent of railways, spoiling the Aube's home sales and leaving the growers totally dependent on the *négociants* of the Marne region. It was when they were at their lowest ebb that these men were stunned to hear the decree of state announcing that the Aube had been excluded from the area entitled to be called Champagne and was forbidden to sell its wines to the Marne. The discontent, which had been simmering, boiled over, to result in such a display of outrage and regional unity as had never been witnessed before in wine history. The Aube had a fierce pride in its past for Troyes had been the centre for medieval Champagne wine fairs and was literally the historic capital. The famous revolt of 1911 followed, bringing administration in the Aube to a grinding halt with strikes, resignations and demonstrations, all organised with perfect control and with the solid backing of the whole of the Aubois people, whose very livelihood was threatened by the decree.

The desired result of this five months of chaos was not to come however until 1927 when the Aube was reintegrated into Champagne – sixteen long years of waiting before those thousands of *vignerons* could once more claim their right to be *champenois*. Mention this event to the older generation and see their reaction; without any knowledge of French you will see how moved they are by the memory of it.

WHERE TO BUY?

To return now to your choice of venue, it is useful to refer back to the remarks about blending. The large Houses have the advantage over the small grower in that they have a good variety of the wine of previous years to blend from; they can also afford to select and buy the particular commune's grapes which they feel will add to their

Les Riceys, part of the attractive Aube region of Champagne

final personal product, for many small growers sell their crop direct to these Houses. The smaller growers have to use just the one year's produce, usually from their own single commune, thus cannot achieve the perfect balance that results from blending; they will have good, bad and indifferent years. You do not however want to pay just for a name, therefore a happy medium is required. Champagne has an unusual system of grading wine communes by which *négociants* pay them a certain percentage of an annually agreed price, those few with 100% rating being the equivalent of Grand Cru, and those with 90-99% qualifying as Premier Cru. The name boards of these communes always let you know if they are in this bracket, so this will be some guide as you tour through; if you choose a grower or firm from a Grand or Premier Cru commune, the chances are that you will be getting a good quality product. Naturally, if you are an accomplished connoisseur of Champagne, your own taste buds are all you need to guide you, but for most of us it is a wine rarely tasted since much of what masquerades in our shops as Champagne is only an inferior 'copy' using similar methods.

The Champagne label differs from those discussed previously, in view of its different vinification. The following words are useful to know if your host does not explain everything clearly at tasting time:

Crémant – only slightly sparkling
Cuvée – blend
Brut, extra sec, sec, demi-sec, doux – from the very dry to the very sweet, according to *dosage*.
Vintage and date – only appears if the blend is of one year's product.
Blanc de Blancs – from the Chardonnay grape only
Rosé – pink Champagne
Réserve – no real meaning

GRAPE VARIETIES
Pinot Noir – grown in the Montagne de Reims
Pinot Meunier – an inferior grape, grown in the valley of the Marne, used in some blends
Chardonnay – the white grape, grown in the Côte des Blancs

Champagne producers look to the Old Testament when it comes to naming the different sizes of bottle!

Magnum – 1½ litres	Methusalen – 6 litres	Balthazar – 12 litres
Jeroboam – 3 litres	Salmanazar – 9 litres	Nebuchadnezzar – 15 litres
Rehoboam – 4½ litres		

NB All Champagne corks have Champagne written on them, all others denote that the wine is not true Champagne.

A FEW FAMOUS HOUSES

In Reims: Mumm, Louis Roederer, Krug, Taittinger, Pommery*, Veuve Clicquot – Ponsardin.

In Épernay: Mercier*, Moët et Chandon*, Pol Roger.

In Ay: Bollinger.

*Cellars of particular interest to tourists.

ADDRESSES

Launois père et fils, 3 av. de la République, le Mesnil sur Oger, 51190 Avize.
100% Grand Cru status, in the Blanc de Blancs region. Good quality/price ratio. Informative visits to cellars, fascinating museum; groups catered for if buffet Champagne meal is required.

Société de Producteurs Mailly-Champagne, 51500 Rilly la Montagne.
100% Grand Cru status. Good quality/price ratio. English spoken during guided visits. Four year stock held. Opening times very accommodating, no crowds or traffic! Personal service.

Mailly-Champagne has its own folklore relating to its formation as a society of producers, beginning in 1929 during the general slump in trade when the Mailly *vignerons* decided to band together and pool their 100% rated harvest into one product. They, like all other individual growers, were having a tough time selling their goods to the big Houses during that difficult period, so, the decision once taken, they built the present premises, including the digging out of the one kilometre of cellars, seventeen metres deep, in their 'spare time' after working all day on their own vineyards. The resulting highly rated Grand Cru Champagne is a tribute to their determination, industry and above all their spirit of co-operation. A model of a typically dressed *vigneron*, complete with pickaxe, is to be seen down in the cellars to remind us all of the story behind this firm, rightly proud of its origins and taking its place now among the greats.

Homage must now be paid to two of Champagne's most legendary figures, both reputed to have contributed greatly to the *méthode champenoise*, Dom Pérignon and the widow (*veuve*) Clicquot. The village of Hautvillers is where you can see the remains of the Abbey where Dom Pérignon was cellar-master until his death in 1715, and where he is said to have experimented profitably with the technique of blending. He is also held responsible for the introduction of the specially reinforced bottle for Champagne, and for the use of corks. Many people think too that he was first to discover how to put the bubbles into the wine, but alas, the English had already beaten him to it, on their home ground! Veuve Clicquot was the clever lady who, a hundred years later, invented the method of *remuage* and *dégorgement* described above. What a messy business it must have been before the freezing method was introduced!

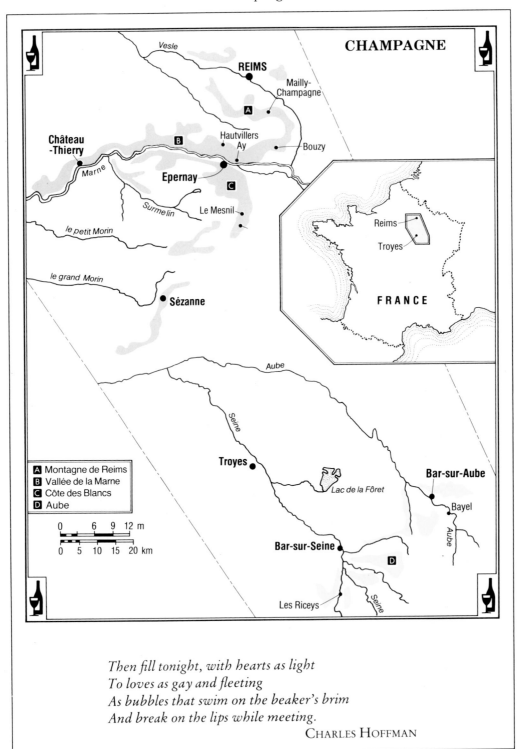

CHAMPAGNE

REIMS

Mailly-Champagne

A

Château -Thierry

B

Hautvillers
Ay

Bouzy

Marne

Epernay

C

Surmelin

Le Mesnil

le petit Morin

le grand Morin

Sézanne

Reims

Troyes

FRANCE

Vesle

Aube

Seine

Troyes

Lac de la Fôret

Bar-sur-Aube

Bayel

Aube

A Montagne de Reims
B Vallée de la Marne
C Côte des Blancs
D Aube

0   6   9   12 m
0   5   10   15   20 km

Bar-sur-Seine

D

Les Riceys

Seine

Then fill tonight, with hearts as light
To loves as gay and fleeting
As bubbles that swim on the beaker's brim
And break on the lips while meeting.

CHARLES HOFFMAN

118

TO SERVE CHAMPAGNE

It should be served cold but not icy, according to most tastes, and merits a special glass to itself, the *flûte*, which can be filled to the brim. In the more open-shaped glasses the precious bubbles disappear too rapidly, which seems sacrilege after they have been nurtured for so long in the cellar. Likewise it seems silly to pop the cork out so that it reaches the ceiling – more bubbles and wine lost! However, let's not moralise, enjoy your Champagne, long may it continue to herald in happy occasions for us all, and if you don't seem to have any coming up soon, do as the French do; they don't need excuses, they open a bottle of their country's most celebrated wine and the occasion follows!

LOCAL PRODUCTS AND SPECIALITIES
Chaource and Mussey cheeses can be found in the Aube.
Fish and game abound on account of the numerous rivers and forests.
Many dishes are cooked in Champagne *nature*, or still wine.
    What about trying the salad of dandelion leaves *(pissenlits)* with sizzling cubes of pork belly, dressed in a piquant vinegar creation?

FURTHER INFORMATION
Comité Régional de Tourisme et des Loisirs,
5 rue de Jericho, 5100 Chalons sur Marne.

Buffet lunch at M. Launois', Champagne flowing freely!

THE JURA
AND SAVOIE

THE JURA

A visit to the Jura mountains is a pure pleasure in itself, particularly when combined with a tour of Alsace. Fortunately the two are connected by the N83 (avoiding the motorway) and the attractive Doubs valley. Of course there is the additional lure of interesting wines to discover in a region which is as yet unspoilt by tourism.

The main wine town, Arbois, was the home of Louis Pasteur, who made his studies on the local grapes in respect of fermentation and diseases of the vine; here the science of oenology was born, according to the local people. One can only wonder what Pasteur would think of the scientific advances today if he were to come back, for nearly every grower employs an oenologist if he has not actually studied oenology himself. Arbois also has rather too many wine shops, so the advice is to explore the neighbouring villages, for it is here that you can get the full flavour and character of the Jura countryside of rolling hills, rambling farmyards, tumbledown hamlets and pretty meadows. Villages are well signposted out of the town and wine routes can be picked up here and there.

Apart from Arbois, the other two regions to search around are L'Étoile and Château Chalon, with the sparkling river Seille nearby and numerous sorties into the *cirques* of this area to be made. But what of the Jura wine, it is very easy in such surroundings to forget all about it. White, rosé, red, *vin jaune* and *vin de paille* are what you can find, the general appellation being Côtes du Jura.

GRAPE VARIETIES
Poulsard or Ploussard – for rosé
Trousseau and Pinot Noir – for reds
Chardonnay and Savagnin – for white
It will be noticed that three unusual varieties are in use here, the Poulsard, Trousseau and Savagnin, all of which are local to the Jura.

Some explanation must be given of the *vin jaune* (yellow wine) and *vin de paille* (straw wine), since these two are unique to the Jura. *Vin jaune* is often called *vin de gelées*, wine of frosts, because it can be very late in the year before the little Savagnin grape is ready for harvest. It gives a very low yield and after fermentation is kept in barrels for approximately six years, with no topping up, until a kind of veil consisting of yeasts has formed over the wine, which in turn give it its yellow colour, its unique flavour and strange aroma. Château Chalon, the tiny village perched picturesquely on top of a hill giving a magnificent view of the plains below, specialises in this wine, the most famous of the Jura. Madame Bury, who told us about this wine, in her dark cellar full of old barrels and odd aromas, showed us the slaty soil on which the wine is grown and explained that this was what accounted for some of the distinctive flavour of the white wines. Château Chalon is reputed to last for a hundred years, she told us proudly, and seemed most loath to part with three bottles, so precious is it to a grower after such a long *élevage*.

ADDRESS
Denis Bury, Château Chalon, Jura.
Wide selection of wines; a most informative visit. Family concern.

Vin de paille also has an interesting upbringing. It is made from a selection of all the grape varieties of the Jura and the bunches of grapes harvested are laid out on beds of straw, hence the name, or more often nowadays, hung up in a clean, airy room, for at least three months. During this time, the grapes dry up and their sugar is concentrated, (compare the *pourriture noble* method), so that the wine which then results after slow fermentation is a *vin doux naturel* (see p.133) with absolutely nothing added to aid the process. It is high in alcohol and is said to act as a tonic, though you'd need to be a rich invalid to take it regularly as medicine!

ADDRESS
Domaine de Montbourgeau, (Jean Gros), L'Étoile 39570 Lons-le-Saunier.
L'Étoile is very pretty to wander through. This domaine is an old family property, with friendly family service.

Pupillin and Montigny-lès-Arsures are two villages neighbouring Arbois which simply must be discovered, so typical are they of this sleepy rural region. The following address is recommended for the whole range of Jura wines carefully brought up according to tradition and all aged in the barrel. Even the *vin de paille* is still left to dry on beds of straw. An intriguing small stack of cobweb-covered 1959 bottles can be picked out if you peer into the gloom behind the barrels – certain wines are not on general sale!

ADDRESS
Roger Lornet, Montigny-lès-Arsures 39600 Arbois.
A young *vigneron* who enjoys explaining his wines to visitors. Tasting among the barrels, wide selection.

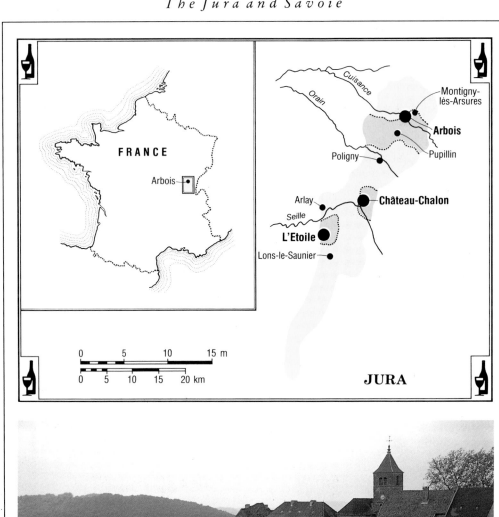

Château Chalon, tiny village perched picturesquely on top of a hill

SAVOIE

The wines of Savoie are little known outside their own area, for they are mostly drunk on the spot in the mountains or by the lakes where they are produced. There is no vast stretch of vines anywhere, not surprisingly in such a region, for vineyards are dotted about in sunny valleys and on well-sited slopes as and when there is space for them. This pattern of cultivation results in the fact that over the whole area entitled to be called Vin de Savoie, the general appellation, there are slight differences to be noted by astute tasters who seek out the Vins de Savoie with a village name added to the label. The wines are mostly white, some slightly *pétillant* and others sparkling, with just a few reds here and there.

The best way is to discover them in passing during the course of enjoying the spectacular scenery, for Lac Léman and Lac du Bourget, both beautiful tourist regions, produce a good number of wines and the rest are never far away. Local grape varieties are much in evidence in the Savoie, whose history, like that of the Jura dates back to Roman times when Pliny the Elder spoke well of its wine.

GRAPE VARIETIES
White: Jacquère, Altesse, Chasselas, Gringet, Bergeron
Red: Gamay, Mondeuse, Pinot

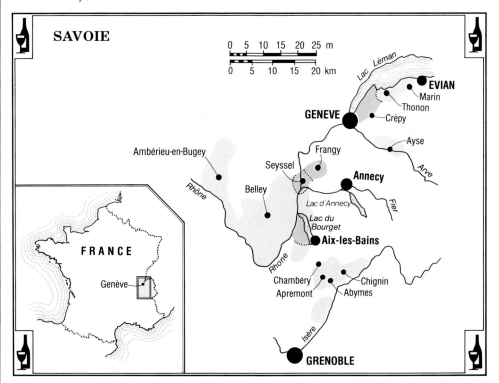

A *route des vins* connects all the interesting areas so if your visit is primarily for wine seeking, this would be a good way to organise it. The main appellations to locate are as follows: Crépy; Seyssel or Seyssel Mousseux; Roussette de Savoie; Vin de Savoie, plus village name.

When not discovering wines you could well be finding cheeses, or better still, combine the two and with some local bread make a meal from them, for the local wines and cheeses often marry together perfectly. Many places on your wine route will also be able to offer visits round the factories, farms or co-operatives where milk products are made, adding an extra dimension to the circuit.

ADDRESS
M. Claude Delalex, Marin, 74200 Thonon les Bains.
By the side of Lac Léman. Not a small venue, but good wines.

Adjoining the Savoie region at its western edge is another area of wine with VDQS status, Bugey. These wines might well be included in a Jura, Savoie, or upper Rhône tour.

BUGEY VDQS

At one time a much more important area of vines, the Bugey region is now very sparse, but represents good hunting ground and family welcomes. Cheeses are also very much in evidence and the discovery of the more remotely made ones can easily vie with wine-seeking for first place.

LOCAL PRODUCTS AND SPECIALITIES
The *charcuterie* shop is where you need to look for Jura specialities, particularly among the variety of hams and sausages.

In the Savoie, you must eat *gratin* dishes, as many different ones as possible. In both regions, the local cheeses are the speciality:

In the Jura, the *Comté*, a *gruyère* cheese is the most famous, but look out also for *Morbier*, remembered for its dark stripe through the middle, the *bleu de Gex* and the *Mont d'Or*.

The *Beaufort*, a Savoie cheese, is a well-known *gruyère* without holes and is used in Savoie *fondue* dishes. *Emmental, Reblochon, Tomme de Savoie* and many others can all be discovered at the *fruitières* and *fromageries* of both regions.

FURTHER INFORMATION

Comité Régional de Tourisme,	Comité Départementale du Tourisme du Jura,
Savoie-Mont Blanc,	Préfecture du Jura,
9 Boulevard Wilson,	39021 Lons-le-Saunier.
73100 Aix les Bain.	

THE SOUTH

This is the part of France which first cultivated vines when, in the sixth century BC, Greek traders sailed to Marseille and began exchanging their goods, using the Rhône as a means of travelling, and fanning out overland to east and west. It was the Romans however, who in the century before Christ, organised the locals into efficient communities and settlements, establishing towns and centres of commerce which today are the very places the tourists flock to – Nîmes, Arles, Aix and Marseille, to name but a few – to see what remains of their buildings and their way of life. It is an area rich in historical interest not only for its Roman origins but also for the fascinating and often gruesome events which took place here during the religious wars and crusades, which have left their mark in the form of castles, forts, towers and hill settlements.

For some, this historical interest, and of course the climate and holiday resorts by the sea, will eclipse the wine interest, for in spite of its important origins the south has not yet made a name for itself in the world at large for fine wines. However, the two interests can combine very naturally as you move about the region, discovering something different every day of both wine and other aspects, for there is nothing if not variety in the south. Furthermore, isn't it so much the better that the world at large has *not* yet found any fine wines, for it leaves the way completely free for us to pioneer them ourselves without treading warily around Grand Crus, Premier Crus and *négociant éleveurs.*

If truth were told, those wine buffs who think there is nothing worth drinking in the south are rather out of touch with the current scene, for the whole vast area has made tremendous strides towards improvement in the last decade or so under the guidance of experts, using modern techniques and better grape varieties.

A glimpse into the background of wine-making in the south soon reveals the reason for many wine-lovers scorning its product. Basically there is an abundance of rich and fertile soil on the plains which results in far too much wine being produced, to very low standards. Efforts were made to induce growers to reduce on quantity but they backfired and even politics came on the scene with many unpleasant repercussions. Now however, real progress is being made, particularly in the hillier areas to the west, in the Languedoc and Roussillon, and a remark made by one vineyard owner in Provence seems perfectly justifiable, 'All Bordeaux and Burgundy wine is not necessarily good, just as all Provence wine is not necessarily bad.' To sum up, there is plenty of good wine to be found at very reasonable prices and our advice is to go out there and find it now before the 'world at large' gets to hear of it.

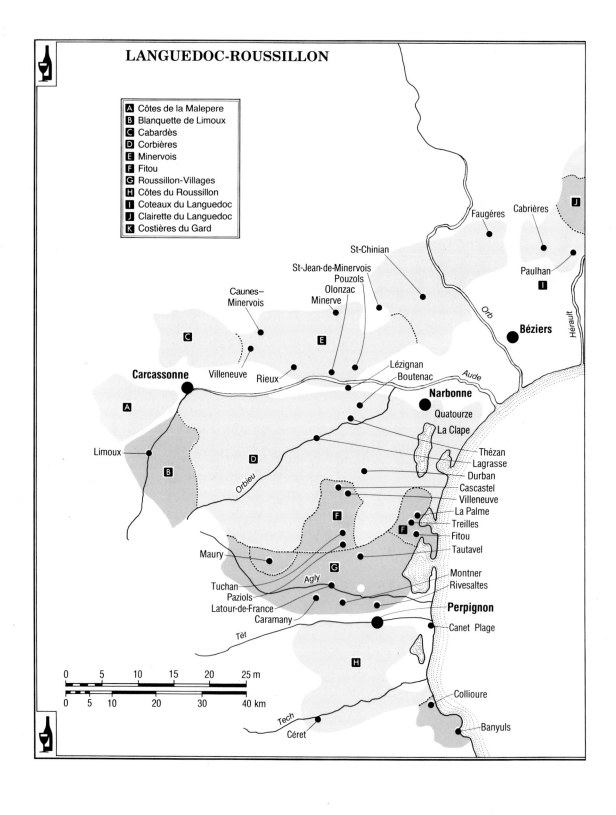

LANGUEDOC-ROUSSILLON

A Côtes de la Malepere
B Blanquette de Limoux
C Cabardès
D Corbières
E Minervois
F Fitou
G Roussillon-Villages
H Côtes du Roussillon
I Coteaux du Languedoc
J Clairette du Languedoc
K Costières du Gard

Faugères
Cabrières
J
St-Chinian
St-Jean-de-Minervois
Pouzols
Olonzac
Caunes–
Minervois
Minerve
Paulhan
I
Béziers
Orb
Hérault
C
E
Villeneuve
Rieux
Lézignan
Boutenac
Aude
Carcassonne
Narbonne
Quatourze
La Clape
A
Thézan
Lagrasse
Limoux
D
Durban
Orbieu
Cascastel
Villeneuve
B
La Palme
Treilles
F
Fitou
F
Tautavel
Maury
Montner
G
Rivesaltes
Agly
Tuchan
Perpignon
Paziols
Latour-de-France
Caramany
Canet Plage
Tèt

0   5   10   15   20   25 m

0   5   10   20   30   40 km

H
Collioure
Tech
Céret
Banyuls

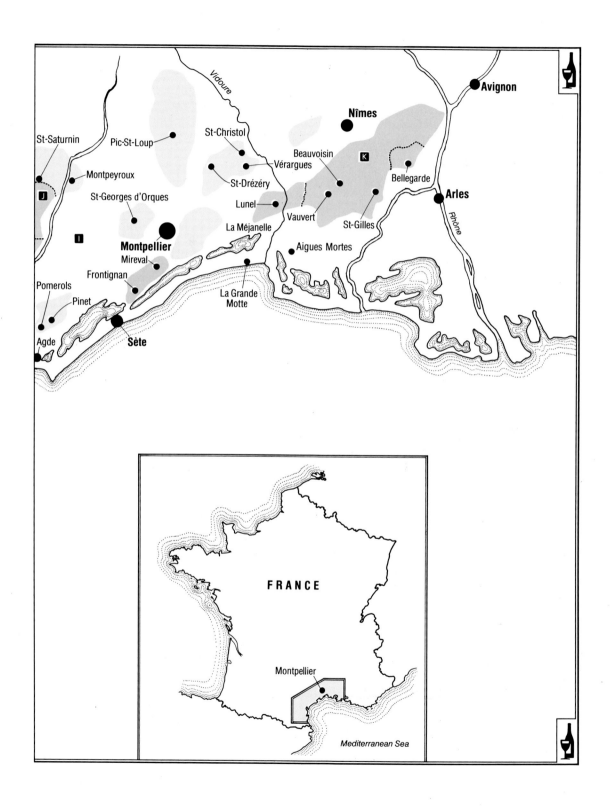

LANGUEDOC

The wines of the Languedoc do not fall neatly into nice blocks, easily documented, but it is proposed to start with the largest areas, each of which contain smaller ACs within their confines. There are five main areas.

MINERVOIS

This region is becoming rapidly well known since the transformation of the coast into holiday resorts, for it is just a nice ride into the hills for holiday-makers who want a break from the sea. Minerve itself warrants a visit, which will quickly open up a further interest in this rugged country, for its story of the crusades against the Cathar heretics can be followed throughout both the Minervois and Corbières regions. Although the Minervois is known for red wine, it makes a full range including a *vin doux naturel* (VDN) rejoicing in the name Muscat de St-Jean-de-Minervois. From the banks of the Aude to the plateaux in the north, its terrain ensures perfect hunting ground for it is the land with everything, medieval hill towns, sparkling little rivers, bare rocks and very few straight roads. Secret vineyards are hard to find in view of the many co-operatives here, but all the more satisfying once unearthed. Go into the back-country and follow the notices – there's no guarantee how far you need to follow, however, that's the fun of this area!

ADDRESS
Domaine de Barroubio, St Jean de Minervois, 34360 St-Chinian.
Tiny hamlet, rustic setting, gîte possibility. Silver medal VDN, also red and a rosé Minervois. Very friendly welcome.

Cabardès VDQS wine is Minervois' western neighbour, but in view of its different geographical position, its wines differ too. A visit to Carcassonne could well include a tasting of the red wine of this region.

GRAPE VARIETIES

Carignan		
Cinsaut		
Grenache Noir	}	Red
Syrah		
Mourvèdre		

Grenache Blanc		
Picpoul		
Bourboulenc	}	White
Macabeu		
Clairette		

Each grower uses his own judgement concerning the proportions of this large number of varieties, to suit his terrain and position; there is also some planting now of the 'noble' varieties used elsewhere in France.

CORBIÈRES

Sparkling and bright in liquid night
Does the wine our goblets gleam in;
With hue as red as the rosy bed
Which a bee would choose to dream in.

CHARLES HOFFMAN

Like Minervois, Corbières was appreciated in Roman times and is now enjoying a well deserved comeback of which it is justifiably proud. The area is well routed, taking the traveller not only through the best wine lands but also within reach of so many other attractions that it becomes difficult to decide what to miss out. The answer is to take time over the discovery of this region, for it spreads from Narbonne on the coast nearly to Carcassonne in the west. Private venues are easy to find and the wine is almost all red, though in view of the diversity of the land, there are differences to discover, for instance, the wine nearest to the sea is much lighter and easier to drink whereas that further inland can have a good ageing capacity. Excellent value for money is the comment most often heard in connection with this up and coming region.

ADDRESS
Château Étang des Colombes,
(M. Gualco),
Cruscades, 11200 Lézignan-Corbières.
Not a small vineyard, but personal friendly service, prize-winning wines and a little museum of old vineyard tools.

FITOU

Fitou has the honour of being the first red wine of Languedoc-Roussillon to receive its AOC and is situated within the Corbières boundaries nearest the sea with one group of communes and in its central part with the other. Its reputation reaches back to the days of Louis XIV and today it is still much admired by locals and tourists alike, especially for its ability to age well, whilst still being very good to drink when young.

   Most of Fitou's growers send their produce to the co-operatives so it is quite difficult to find a private venue, but they do exist if you are determined enough to seek one out. The co-operative below makes Corbières also and all Fitou communes have the right to produce the VDN Rivesaltes too.

ADDRESS
Cave Co-opérative de Paziols, 11530 Paziols.
Typical co-operative premises with shop for tasting and buying.

COTEAUX DU LANGUEDOC

This is an area very difficult to delineate, but offering interesting discoveries. The best method for the wine enthusiast to find his way about it is provided by a leaflet prepared by the growers themselves. It offers us six different routes covering the whole varied area, taking into account not only the wines but sites of local interest too.

La Route Bleue – Quatourze and La Clape
Quatourze has red and rosé, as do most of these little districts, but La Clape makes an unusual style white wine also, in conjunction with its good strong red.
La Route des Schistes – St-Chinian and Faugères
These two qualify for their own ACs and have pride in this fact.
La Route de Molière – Cabrières, Clairette du Languedoc, Picpoul de Pinet.
The Clairette area gives us a dry white wine, having its own AC and using the

Clairette grape, whereas Picpoul de Pinet is also white but takes its name from the Picpoul grape; it would be interesting to compare the two perhaps. Cabrières is a tiny area within Clairette in very attractive countryside and we would recommend the visitor to ignore the rather impersonal co-operative there and locate the address below. Apart from having excellent wine, it is an absolute pleasure to find, being 3½ km. off an already minor road in a delightful hidden valley, full of broom in the right season – a veritable secret vineyard, yet giving us a little signpost to help us in the right direction.

ADDRESS
Domaine du Temple, (Maurice Muller),
Cabrières 34800 Clermont-l'Hérault.
Prize-winning wines, a firm believer in quality not quantity. Even the *vin de pays* is remarkable!

La Route des Garrigues – St-Saturnin and Montpeyroux
As the name implies we are into moorland up here, with the scent of herbs to add to the pleasure of finding two more wines.
La Route des Guilhem – La Méjanelle, St-Georges-d'Orques, Pic-St-Loup
The first two of these districts surround Montpellier, home of French viticulture, and are much loved by its residents. Try the third when admiring the panorama from the Pic.
La Route de la Bouvine – St-Drézéry, St-Christol, Vérargues
On the Nîmes/Montpellier route, not far from the Camargues, this route also includes one of the south's VDNs, Muscat de Lunel (see p.133) which can be tasted and bought at any of the roadside booths around this area. Just west of Montpellier, by the sea, are two others at Frontignan and Mireval, the former better known than the latter.

COSTIÈRES DU GARD

A *route des vins* is already in operation for this recently earned appellation, which combines well with a visit to the impressive Pont du Gard. The area benefits from a pebbly soil *(grès)*, which helps to keep all the heat long after the sun has gone down. Its main production is red.

ADDRESS
Cave Co-opérative Costières de Beauvoisin,
Av. de la Gare, 30640 Beauvoisin.
A union of three Beauvoisin producers. Very friendly welcome and a very brisk trade locally at reasonable prices, wide range of wines available.

CLAIRETTE DE BELLEGARDE

A tiny area within the Costières producing white wines. Like the Clairette du Languedoc, it used to be criticised for being flat and uninteresting, but these wines too are making a new reputation for themselves thanks to modern technology.

BLANQUETTE DE LIMOUX

Blanquette de Limoux is the oldest sparkling wine in France, the monks at St-Hilaire near to Limoux being known to have produced it as early as 1531. It has the distinction too of being the only *mousseux* wine produced in the Languedoc/ Roussillon and uses the unusual (for this area) grape, the Mauzac, with a little Chardonnay and Chenin added. The *champenois* method is widely used but there is also much advertising of 'ancestral' or 'traditional' methods, whereby a wine is produced which is easy on the stomach and is not likely to give headaches. A still white wine is also made, called Vin de Blanquette, but it is the sparkling one which has been making great strides in quality recently. The town is a little marred by signs for Blanquette as one approaches, but we found a perfectly situated private grower in the countryside just a few miles away.

ADDRESS
Robert, Domaine de Fourn, Pieusse 11300 Limoux.
An old family firm, totally surrounded by its vines, with a good variety of wines right down to *vin de pays*.

Bordering Blanquette is an interesting VDQS region, Côtes de la Malepère using a different blend of grape varieties which produces a red wine going well with the local *cassoulet*.

Before leaving the Languedoc wines to embark on a journey into the Roussillon, it seems appropriate here to mention the sweet wine which these two areas are both well known for, the *vin doux naturel* as it is termed.

VIN DOUX NATUREL

The term seems to be a misnomer for 'sweet natural wine' is in fact fortified by the addition of brandy. This, added during the course of fermentation, stops the sugar from fermenting further since sugar cannot do so after a certain strength of alcohol has been reached. The result is a very sweet wine of high alcohol content, usually around 18 degrees.

GRAPE VARIETIES
Muscat – used on its own for all VDNs called Muscat de. . . .
Grenache ⎫
Malvoisie ⎬ in varying proportions for all other VDNs.
Macabeo ⎭

The yield of the Muscat grape is very small and the wines are aged for a good long period before being released, thus resulting in a product which is more expensive than the other wines of the region. Each appellation has its own particular characteristics arising from its mix of grape varieties, its position and soil, and its ageing methods.

THE ROUSSILLON

The Roussillon is attracting much attention recently as the results of the drive towards improvement mentioned at the beginning of this chapter are starting to show, particularly in the red wines which are strong and rich-coloured. Many growers now make part of their harvest into a quicker-maturing easy to enjoy wine by the carbonic maceration techniques used in the Beaujolais for example, but they also make wine which is not bottled until two years have elapsed and which reaches 12 degrees of alcohol, thus giving the customer a choice. Some wine is even put into new oak barrels for a time in order to give it a special 'something' much sought after by lovers of classical red.

CÔTES DU ROUSSILLON

This is the most southerly of Roussillon's vineyards, sharing the land with large areas of fruit, particularly peaches and apricots. The eastern Pyrenees provide a beautiful backdrop of scenery which makes travelling a pure pleasure, especially in the region of the foothills where you can pick out routes which combine everything, vines, fruits, historic towns, and mountains.

CÔTES DU ROUSSILLON-VILLAGES

This is the northerly part merging into Corbières and including twenty-five communes which are entitled to add *'villages'* to the appellation on the label. These are the best of the Roussillon wines, all red, having more body and the ability to age well, and out of these, two so far have the right to add their specific name, Caramany and Latour-de-France. As elsewhere in this southern corner, private growers exist but are hard to find, most of the smaller ones contributing their produce to the local co-operative.

ADDRESS
Les Vignerons de Latour-de-France,
Société Co-opérative Vinicole,
2 av. Général de Gaulle, 66720 Latour-de-France.
A wide range of local wine here, as well as its being the only source for Latour-de-France AC.

RIVESALTES VDN

The area named Rivesaltes borders the Côtes du Rousillon and produces the largest quantity of all the VDN appellations, growing its vines on the poor parched ground which they love, the hotter the better! Mostly it is white, but it can be made of Grenache Noir into a richly-coloured wine too, which we noticed at our venue being sold *en vrac* and being highly recommended by the local people. Muscat de Rivesaltes is to drink young, often accompanying desserts.

ADDRESS
As above, at Latour-de-France. It is sold here in three varieties.

The Banyuls vineyards literally fall into the sea . . .

COLLIOURE

This is a tiny appellation for red wines only, occupying four communes along the coast, which then give way to Spanish territory, Port Vendres, Banyuls and Cerbère being the other three. It is a picturesque little port, at its best in the early morning before the holiday-makers arrive to enjoy its beaches and water sports activities.

BANYULS

Banyuls is the most familiar name of the four, well known for its VDN wine, said to be the best of all of them, and produced in all four communes. The special position of these vineyards at Banyuls, which literally fall into the sea, the poor soil on which the vines grow, the sun striking the steep terraces and the influence of the Mediterranean all account for the fact that the grapes are full of sugar and interesting aromas. A *route du vin* for the intrepid in light vehicles only provides a glimpse of the work which goes into the growing of this crop. In places the terraces only hold two or three rows of vines, they are shored up with supporting walls and are composed of stones as far as the untrained eye can see. The vines are knotty and twisted, clinging on obstinately as they have for centuries and the *vignerons* here have no option but to work manually.

The wines must reach a minimum of 22 degrees of alcohol and are kept in the wood for at least thirty months if they are Grand Cru standard, and often much longer according to what style of wine is required.

Many areas of vines appear to have been abandoned around Banyuls, making the visitor wonder whether the tourist industry is perhaps more lucrative, for holiday homes and flats are springing up everywhere along the coast. However, the wine is readily available at numerous roadside booths, many of them featuring on panoramic lay-bys using huge barrels to provide an attractive presentation, and in the town itself in rather the same way that fish and chip shops occur in English seaside resorts.

ADDRESS
Domaine du Mas Blanc, (Parcé et fils),
9 av. du Général de Gaulle,
66650 Banyuls sur Mer.
Here is Collioure AC as well as a good selection of Banyuls.

Though it is not the intention to dictate routes to travellers, there is one which simply must be recommended for it combines so many of the wines mentioned above with every aspect of the Roussillon's scenery, including some vivid memorials to its historic past. Starting at Banyuls, head for Roman Céret by the most scenic route and from there wend your way via Thuir, Millas and Latour-de-France through to Maury, where another famous VDN is to be found. The Château de Queribus is a must here for those intrigued by Cathar history, after which the Agly river and its gorges can be followed through to Couiza. Limoux could follow, after which it would not be far to Carcassonne. If this is your first visit to the area it would be a magnificent introduction to its wines and countryside.

PROVENCE

With crimson juice the thirsty southern sky
Sucks from the hills where buried armies lie,
So that the dreamy passion it imparts
Is drawn from heroes' bones and lovers' hearts
O. W. HOLMES

Provence, land of herbs and flowers and home of modern art, has many attractions which would seem to outclass those of its wines, with its reputation for high-living holidays, private yachts and film stars, but it is nevertheless a vast region of vineyards which reaches right down to the seashore and goes far into the foothills inland. In fact it is the tourist industry which has helped to put Provence's wines back on the map, for although they date back as far as the settlers who arrived at Marseille six centuries before the time of Christ, they have suffered from not being on any well-worn major routes. They also suffered from a poor reputation until the great surge of interest in improved techniques and better grape varieties recently made its mark and holidaying wine-lovers with an inquiring nature began to discover many hitherto unknown qualities and wine types.

The vineyards divide into two major areas, the Côtes de Provence and the Coteaux d'Aix, with one or two tiny appellations either included within them or attached, except for Bellet, a tiny outpost whose wines seem to find their place in the Nice restaurants among the local dishes.

CÔTES DE PROVENCE

This area covers both the coast and the hillier terrain inland, so the tourist need not really go much further than his beach in order to find good wine. It seems incredible that some of the best should be not far inland from St Tropez itself, the Château de Minuty being one well-known source nearby. The coastal route combines the rugged scenery of the Maures outcrop with the local colourful seaside resorts, the famous Provence light promoting the sale of sunglasses and camera film, but if you want to leave all this behind for a while, follow the wine route up through the Maures and along what is often termed the high road, in the direction of Draguignan. The cork oak trees used in the bottle cork industry can be seen throughout the Maures mountains, and chestnut trees provide the source for the local *marrons glacés* and other delicious products. Further inland the scenery changes and olive trees become very much in evidence, often growing side by side with the vines. There are plenty of vines but not always plenty of private domaines, or *mas*, as they are often called in Provence for, as usual when the custom is to own small plots of land, the co-operatives are in full swing. Secret vineyards are always there however, if only you can take the time to enjoy stumbling across one and, if the one we found is anything to go by, they have a few surprises in store for those who think that all Provence wine is rosé and mediocre, fit only for quaffing with beach picnics. A *route de vins* will guide you through the best areas for hunting down good wine, but it's necessary to take a side road occasionally to find interesting terrain.

Our recommended venue is at Correns, where the local co-operative names its wines after the Croix de Basson, an enormous cross on top of a hill overlooking the village. Legend tells us that in the days when indulgences were bought, a returning crusader put up the cross in exchange for the pardoning of his sins, and in the village church even to this day, on the Friday nearest May 3rd, everyone who passes through the *Porte du Pardon* that day is forgiven his sins. Today it is a colourful folklore event, but in the Middle Ages, this *Pardon* was taken most seriously.

ADDRESS
Domaine des Aspras, (Lisa Latz), Correns, near Carcès.
Lady owner speaks good English. The white wine of this area is her speciality, but a whole range is offered.

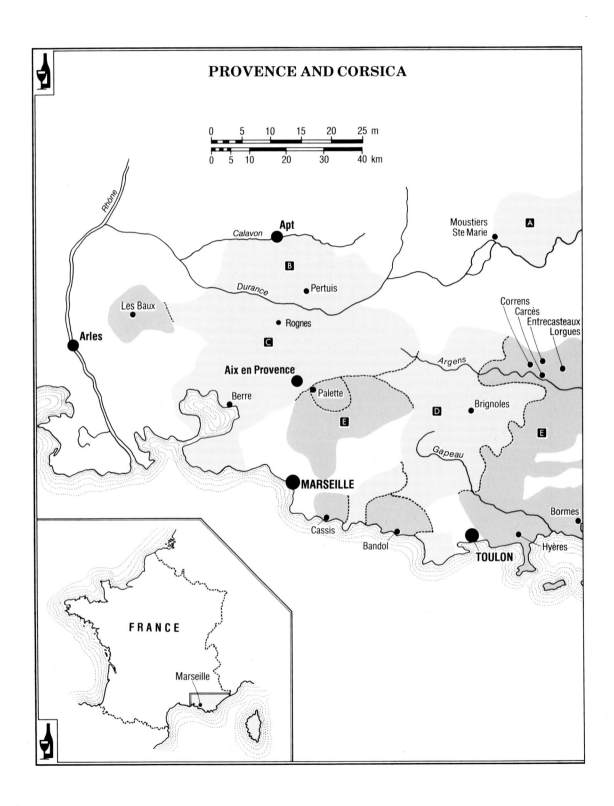

PROVENCE AND CORSICA

0 5 10 15 20 25 m

0 5 10 20 30 40 km

Rhône

Calavon **Apt**

Moustiers
Ste Marie   A

B

Durance   • Pertuis

Les Baux   Correns
                  Carcès
• Rognes   Entrecasteaux
C   Lorgues

Arles

Argens

Aix en Provence

Berre   Palette   Brignoles

              E   D   E

Gapeau

MARSEILLE

                    Bormes

Cassis   Bandol   **TOULON**   Hyères

FRANCE

Marseille

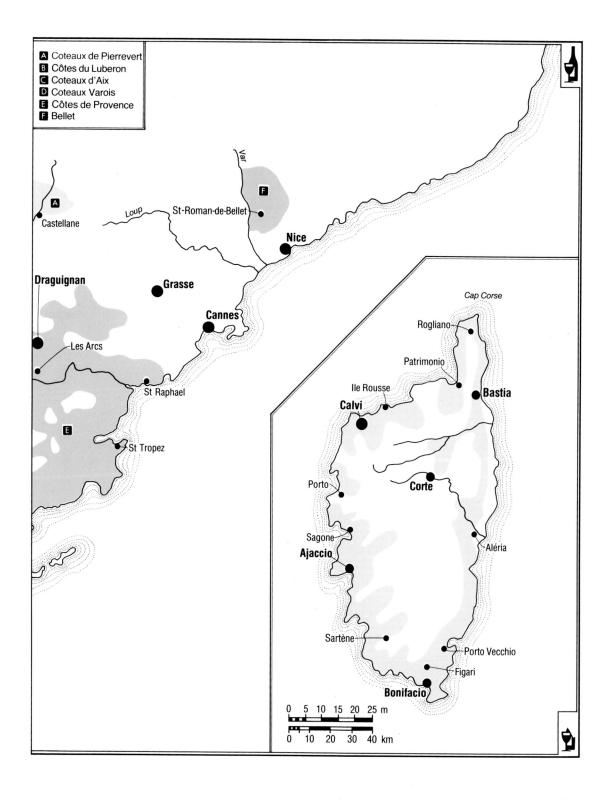

A Coteaux de Pierrevert
B Côtes du Luberon
C Coteaux d'Aix
D Coteaux Varois
E Côtes de Provence
F Bellet

A
Castellane

Loup
Var
St-Roman-de-Bellet
F

Nice

Draguignan
Grasse
Cannes

Les Arcs

St Raphael

E

St Tropez

Cap Corse
Rogliano

Patrimonio

Ile Rousse
Calvi
Bastia

Porto

Corte

Sagone
Ajaccio

Aléria

Sartène

Porto Vecchio

Figari

Bonifacio

0 5 10 15 20 25 m

0 10 20 30 40 km

From Draguignan it is not very far to the Gorges du Verdon, which have the reputation of being Europe's answer to the Grand Canyon, and deservedly so. Moustiers, famous for its pottery, is also a starting point at the other end of the canyon and could well be combined with tasting the Coteaux de Pierrevert wines, which strictly speaking belong to the Rhône. At Moustiers we come across another interesting background story to do with the golden star suspended across the chasm under which Moustiers nestles. The star was erected there by a knight returning from the crusades in fulfilment of a vow made during his captivity. The setting of the little town in these rocks is incredible; suddenly out of the scrublands of thyme and lavender there rears a mass of steep cliffs, with dwellings clinging on precariously, the star clearly visible from far away.

Lest I appear to be digressing, I hasten to add that the further away from the coast the traveller explores, the more interesting the land becomes and there is always wine to find en route to justify the journey if needs be. VDQS Côtes du Luberon are found on the right bank of the Durance, whereas those on the left are part of the Coteaux d'Aix. The VDQS Coteaux Varois are scattered about the Var, but concentrated most in the Brignoles area between the two large appellations.

COTEAUX D'AIX EN PROVENCE

The town of Aix itself with its Roman history and the fact that Cézanne's home and workplace is not far away is usually enough to attract the tourist, but of course there is wine too! Best known for its reds and rosés, the Coteaux d'Aix can surprise us with a white too occasionally. Hunting is best done away from the tourist areas in the wide open spaces dotted with unvisited *villages perchés*, or hill towns, through lavender and thyme-scented *garrigue*. The position of these fascinating settlements is accounted for by the fact that it was necessary during Provence's early period to protect the occupants as far as possible from enemy attack. Many of the original villages are now unoccupied, but remains of their walls and gates can still be spotted.

COTEAUX DES BAUX EN PROVENCE

This is one of the said tourist areas of course and, without its coachloads and souvenir shops, Les Baux would be a sheer delight to explore, situated as it is in the midst of such an unexpected outcrop of rock, the Alpilles. Alas it is ruined by commerce, but there are nine choices of venue in the neighbourhood if you want to try the wine. Olives and olive oil are everywhere on sale too in this area and can be bought from the growers direct as opposed to the shops.

ADDRESS
Mas de la Dame, rte de St Rémy, Les Baux de Provence 13520 Maussane.
Prize-winning wines *typé* of the area and Van Gogh interest – he painted this *mas*,
fascinated by its situation and the Provençal light.

CASSIS AND BANDOL

Cassis is the little fishing town not far from Marseille noted for its white wines in particular and for its pretty situation reached via steep roads; its fjords or *calanques*, a great source of beauty, can best be explored by boat. What better way to try the wine of Cassis could there be than with the fishy specialities on the spot? Be warned however, the price of its white can be nearly four times as much as that of the Côtes wines up in the hills and there seems to be no difference in quality to many.

Bandol is known for its red wine, good and strong, which is grown on the terraces, sheltered as is all the coast vineyard from the Mistral wind. It has a good aptitude for ageing several years, unlike most of the Provençal wines which are best drunk young and fresh, but like the Cassis is much more expensive. The discerning wine hunter must decide for himself whether to stay by the pretty coast or head for the wide open spaces and hills!

CORSICA

Corsica's wines come third, after Napoleon and the wild beauty of the island. However, if holiday-makers take the time to leave the beaches or mountain *maquis*, heavily scented with herbs, they might like to hunt down some Patrimonio rosé at the northern end of the island, or the dessert wines made at Cap Corse. Sartène and its villages will offer a powerful red wine; be warned, these wines are high in alcohol. Much wine is imported during poor years to meet the island's own demands, so choose from the appellation areas only if you want to be sure of what you are drinking; individual growers are to be discovered here and are probably the best people to buy from.

GRAPE VARIETIES
Niellucio ⎱ the most widely used varieties of Corsican grapes, in
Sciacarello ⎰ conjunction with others.

LOCAL PRODUCTS AND SPECIALITIES
Cassoulet in the Languedoc is a must and, just remember, it is a serious business here, there is even a club for its followers, the Compagnons du Cassoulet!

Try the Catalan specialities in the Roussillon.

Fish, all along the coast and of course in Corsica, is naturally going to be very

The Coteaux d'Aix, dotted with *villages perchés*

good. *Bouillabaisse* is a kind of stew with surprises, as is *bourride*. There is *langouste à la sètoise*, the lobster dish from Sète, and of course anchovies get into various dishes such as *pissaladière*, a kind of pizza.

Any food *à la provençale* will ensure lots of tomatoes, basil and garlic, and *aïoli* comes with just about everything – a mayonnaise with a difference.

Corsica's speciality, unfortunately, comes from blackbirds which in turn have fed on the berries of the *maquis – pâté de merle*.

FURTHER INFORMATION
For Languedoc-Roussillon: Comité Régional de Tourisme,
12 rue Foch,
3400 Montpellier

For Provence-Alpes-Côte d'Azur: Comité Régional de Tourisme,
22a rue Louis Maurel,
13006 Marseille

THE LOIRE VALLEY

The term Loire Valley is used for the sake of convenience to describe what are really four main regions of wine, widely differing in situation and character but all having the river Loire meandering through their midst. Variety is the key word used in connection with its wines and it is this, coupled with the wide appeal of the region for tourists, which makes it one of the most popular holiday resorts in France. In terms of wine hunting and secret vineyards it represents fruitful ground for exploration for, although there are a few 'great' wines to be found, the Loire's produce is generally termed 'very pleasant' or 'charming', thus allowing the visitor to enjoy tasting wherever he goes without feeling obliged to gaze in awe at any particular château or to appreciate the noble characteristic of anything vastly expensive.

The most commonly used words for describing its wines can equally be applied to the countryside of the Loire for it is indeed charming and a delight to discover – frequently called the garden of France in its tourist brochures. The Loire valley is admittedly full of tourists in the high season, but there is absolutely no need to stay on the well-worn routes in order to find either wine or other attractions; many of the tributaries of the Loire open up little-frequented areas where good quality wine is easily found, including some that many people have not heard of. Nearly all the regions we mention below offer a well signed wine route off the main roads, and when the traffic is whooshing along elsewhere, you can often have whole areas of peaceful beauty to yourselves where there is always something of interest round the corner, but no queue to get near it!

Vines were cultivated as early as Roman times and, as in most other parts of France, the Church exerted a great influence on the vineyards, its members passing on both skills and zeal to the local peasants. England had strong connections with Touraine, and Anjou in particular, during the Middle Ages in that our kings were also counts of Anjou, and wine used to be brought down the Loire to be shipped to England from Nantes. Alas, Bordeaux beckoned in subsequent years and our beloved claret eclipsed the Loire wines for ever. Recently however, we are seeing more of these regional wines on our menus and in our shops, which should make it doubly interesting to go and see for ourselves what the 'genuine article' is like. This lure, plus

143

the fact that there are several regions of little known wine to find out about must place a visit to the Loire high on the wine-hunting priority list.

MUSCADET

Muscadet wine has recently become very popular both in France and abroad, with exports to England going from strength to strength. To discover its wines as well as its countryside, two wine routes have been planned out, one for the Muscadet region itself and one for the Gros Plant VDQS region, which overlaps but is generally speaking nearer to the sea. The best Muscadet is considered to come from the Sèvre et Maine area which is bordered to the south west by the 'plain' Muscadet appellation and to the north-east by Muscadet des Coteaux de la Loire. It is an essentially dry white wine, intended to be drunk young and fresh.

GRAPE VARIETIES
Muscadet (local name Melon)
Gros Plant (local name Folle Blanche) – for VDQS wine
Gamay – for Ancenis VDQS red and rosé

You are scarcely out of the city of Nantes, heading in the Clisson/Poitiers direction before you find yourself in vines which look most incongruous next to factories, but it is here that the wine route through Sèvre et Maine can be picked up. It takes you through all the most interesting areas as well as the main vineyards, ending at Clisson, a pretty little town on the river, known for the Italian influence on its architecture. Buying is easy for there are plenty of signs for *vente directe* bordering the route. The term *sur lie* appears on these signs occasionally which warrants a brief explanation. The wines must have spent only one winter in the barrel and must be put into bottles straight 'off the lees', or dead yeasts, which accounts for extra freshness and bouquet and a slight tingling sensation on the tongue.

Best areas: Saint-Fiacre, La Haie Fouassière, Le Pallet

ADDRESS
Domaine des Noelles de Sèvre, (Chereau et fils),
34 rue de la Poste 44690 Monnières.
For Sèvre et Maine and Gros Plant. Family firm. The church in the village has 'wine-making' windows!

The Coteaux d'Ancenis VDQS wines pave the way next for their red and rosé neighbours of Anjou.

ANJOU/SAUMUR

This region divides neatly into several smaller ones, whose wines display individual characteristics according to grapes used, the soil they grow on and the methods of vinification. The most widely exported wine, to England at least, is the rosé d'Anjou, but take a look at the list below, and you will realise how much you might have been missing, had you not come; it is a brief guide intended to help the tourist organise his wine around the rest of his activities.

Red – Saumur and its neighbouring villages in the direction of Tours. Saumur-Champigny is the name to look for on the label. Several wine routes guide you around the area.

ADDRESS
Domaine Filliatreau, Chaintres, Dampierre sur Loire, Saumur.
This family firm cannot keep up with demand!

Dry white – Savennières. Coulée de Serrant and La Roche aux Moines are the best vineyards, in the Coteaux de la Loire region.

ADDRESS
Château de la Roche aux Moines, (Mme. Joly), 49170 Savennières.
Gracious welcome. Wine in class of its own but expensive.

Sweet wine – Coteaux du Layon with its six communes entitled to add their name to the label. Quarts de Chaume and Bonnezeaux outstanding.

ADDRESS
Domaine du Petit Metris, (Renou Robin), 49190 St-Aubin de Luigné.
Very friendly welcome. The whole range of Anjou wines made. Chaume and Quarts de Chaume a speciality.

Rosé – Appears to be made over the whole area and comes in three forms:
Cabernet d'Anjou – considered the best, semi-sweet
Rosé d'Anjou – semi sweet
Rosé de Loire – dry

Sparkling – Saumur. The official general name is Crémant de Loire. The wine gains its sparkling tendencies from the tufa on which it grows. A visit to the cellars in Saumur is a must to see how the Champagne method is applied. (See p.112, Champagne chapter). Also around Saumur are mushroom cellars which can be visited and many different styles of rock dwellings, making fascinating touring between wine stops.

Fontevraud Abbey is not far away, conveniently placed on the Saumur/Champigny wine route, a place of outstanding historic interest, particularly for English people.

The above gives a guide to the best areas for each wine type but there are many other hunting grounds which will yield up treasure if we care to wander away from the main wine and sight-seeing routes. Two rivers, the Aubance and the Loir (without an 'e') are just waiting to be discovered, both areas having wines of high quality.

COTEAUX DE L'AUBANCE

The river is only a stream really, but it offers a neat area for exploration, just north of the more visited Layon, and its wines are typical of Anjou. A new road has caused the villages to be rather cut off and the whole area is pleasantly low-key, with hardly any notices in sight except near Brissac, its largest town, which boasts a beautiful château, not to be missed.

ADDRESS
Moget, l'Homois, St-Jean des Mauvrets.
Family vineyard, friendly welcome, a good range of wine made and stocked.

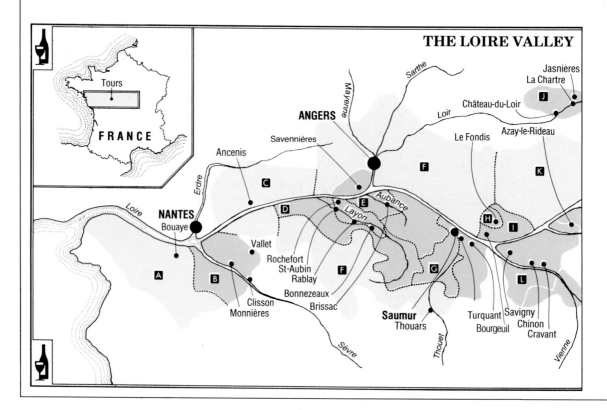

The château at Brissac, open to the public

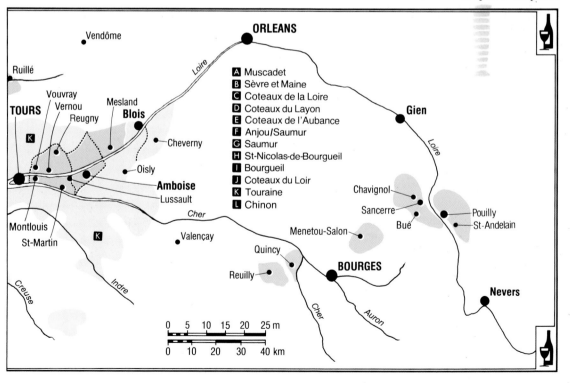

A Muscadet
B Sèvre et Maine
C Coteaux de la Loire
D Coteaux du Layon
E Coteaux de l'Aubance
F Anjou/Saumur
G Saumur
H St-Nicolas-de-Bourgueil
I Bourgueil
J Coteaux du Loir
K Touraine
L Chinon

COTEAUX DU LOIR AND JASNIÈRES

The river Loir could be considered to be a smaller version of the busy Loire to the south, for it has plenty for the tourist to see including the famous Le Lude château, and even has the tufa rock dwellings along one side of the road, just as the road beyond Saumur, yet there are not nearly so many tourists. The wines of this area are either white, similar to those of Vouvray, or light reds; the Coteaux du Loir is fairly easy to find, but Jasnières we found to be elusive to say the least! Though there is such a place on a good map, it didn't ever appear on a signpost, but undaunted I asked a man busy demolishing an old cottage if he could send me to a grower of Jasnières. No, he said, the only one he knew was in hospital, but on seeing my disappointed face, he ventured to say that the bottle he was actually drinking from in the middle of all the dust and rubble was Jasnières and, if I wasn't too particular about the venue, he would give me a *dégustation!* We joined him and his two labourers at a filthy old table, due for demolition, toasted each other's health with dry Jasnières in dubious beakers and had a great time discussing wine; it must rank as the most unusual secret vineyard surely.

ADDRESS
Philippe Sevault, Jasnières – wherever that is!
When the weather has been favourable, Jasnières can produce a sweet wine comparable to those of the Loire, but more attractively priced. We challenge you to find it – we are still looking ourselves!

Elsewhere in the well-known area of Anjou, wine is easily available; the difficulty is rather in deciding which venue to choose. A rule of thumb for us would be to ignore the ones with the biggest, gaudiest adverts and take time to find those growers who will have time for *you*. It was on one such quest that we screeched to a halt, having spotted something which we thought no longer existed, a heavy horse working up and down the rows of vines. Photographs led to chatting which in turn led us to returning at the end of the day to a spot we would never have found, for it is not advertised. If you visit the Coteaux du Layon, and the vines around Rochefort, you might be lucky too in seeing Katie at work, toiling placidly up and down, one man guiding her, the other handling the harrows. The results of her work were noticeably far better than that done on the neighbouring patch by machine.

GRAPE VARIETIES

Chenin Blanc (Pinot de la Loire locally) – for best whites	Groslot or Grolleau
	Gamay } – for other rosé
Cabernet Franc – for best red and rosé	Cot (or Malbec)

148

TOURAINE

As with Anjou, we begin by noting which wine-styles are at their best in which areas to help you orientate your course through this lovely section of the Loire, where magnificent châteaux seem to rise up around every bend in the river.
Chinon and Bourgueil – Red
Vouvray and Montlouis, producing sweet, dry and sparkling – White

CHINON AND BOURGUEIL

Chinon lies on the river Vienne, thus giving you a good excuse for branching off 'the main road' which so many tourists seem glued to, at either side of the river. The writer Rabelais, a former inhabitant and wine lover, has bequeathed to his local wine the description of 'taffeta' – see if you agree with him or can come up with something equally poetic of your own! Bourgueil and St-Nicholas-de-Bourgueil are at the other side of the Loire, also away from the main road, but the two appellations are near enough to be tried during the one tour, giving you the chance to make your own comparisons.

ADDRESS
Jean Delanoue, Le Fondis, St-Nicholas-de-Bourgueil.
Very friendly welcome, family concern.
This grower was kind enough to show us his cellar which is typical of that of all those growers living in this special area of tufa. The entrance was hidden, no-one could have guessed that miles and miles of similar labyrinthine caves and passages lie underneath the roads and fields for as far as this chalky terrain goes. His particular cellar was only a small one he said casually, as we drove on through endless unlit tunnels and arches, and was once used for mushroom growing. Before that, it was quarried, providing the golden stones of which so many of the local houses and châteaux are built.

VOUVRAY

The great sweet wines of Vouvray also enjoy these underground cellars and the greatest of them could happily sit there for fifty years or more for they are renowned for their long life. Vouvray also makes a dry white and a sparkling wine in two forms, slightly sparkling or *pétillant* and *mousseux*.

When approaching Vouvray from the riverside road, we were surprised on our first visit to see no vines and thought we had been dreaming it all up, but sure enough it's all there for the seeking, higher up than expected, much of it reached by the Vallée

The tufa cellars at Bourgeuil, secret entrances, underground arches, mould-covered barrels and labyrinthine passages

Coquette, a road leading up into the slopes where a wine route can eventually be followed. The town is interesting to explore for here as elsewhere the rocks and cliffs provide homes and storage space for many of its inhabitants – we even saw a dog kennel built into the rocks and hoped it was well lined in winter! Of course, it must not be forgotten that the chief use of the rocks in this region is that of cellars, for they give exactly the right temperature for wine storage and also ensure that there is no strong light, one of the other essentials for keeping wines in good condition.

ADDRESS
J. C. Aubert, La Vallée Coquette, 37210 Vouvray.
Tasting in the kind of cellar typical of this area.

MONTLOUIS

Montlouis at the opposite side of the river from Vouvray has similar wines but lower prices, so if you enjoy what you taste here, why go further? There are plenty of venues to choose from, nearly all of them being represented at the local *Cave Touristique* which is a large cellar organised by the Montlouis growers for promoting their wines and educating the public in general about wine-growing. The visitor can wander around the museum of wine implements then try whichever wines he fancies. Unlike the unions, this *Cave* (and there are many such in the Loire), offers a sample of all the growers' individual production and quite often the result is that the visitor then follows up the address for the wine he liked and pays a personal visit.

ADDRESS
Alain Joulin, 2, rue Traversière, St-Martin le Beau, Montlouis.
Fantastic rock cellars, very pleasant welcome. Variety of wines.

TOURAINE-AZAY-LE-RIDEAU

Whilst château visiting in Touraine you ought to take time off for a little wine hunting too, and here at Azay-le-Rideau you can combine the two very successfully. This commune is one of three, the others being Mesland and Amboise, which qualify to add their name to Touraine.

ADDRESS
Robert Denis, 11, rue de la Rabière, La Chapelle-Sainte-Blaise, Azay-le-Rideau.
M. Denis and his wife work their vineyard together without help. A very warm welcome and excellent wines. A little English spoken.

Here in the cellar at Azay, we heard that since the finding of Gallo-Roman remains of a press in 1950, poor old St Martin of Tours has lost his claim to have started it all off in Touraine; Azay's vineyard is now definitely known to be the oldest. The history of the Grolleau, the grape used here for its dry rosé is interesting, for it is only tolerated elsewhere in Touraine, yet here it is recommended. It was discovered by chance in 1500 only 8 km from Azay, when its use spread throughout Anjou and Touraine, but it was not highly favoured since it is a generous grape and only gives a wine weak in alcohol. It was abandoned by everyone else, but in Azay they do things their own way and have always practised *taille courte*, or strict pruning, and thus have concentrated the strength of the resulting wine and continue to use their local grape proudly.

Throughout the whole of this region, the Touraine Sauvignon in particular is gaining in popularity, one of its best spots being at Oisly, where you will find a choice of growers.

CHEVERNY VDQS

Moving out of Touraine a little, but still in pursuit of historic castles, we can discover another unusual grape, the Romorantin, which is grown nowhere else in such quantity; it is the local white grape of Cheverny. The castle at Cheverny is best known for its beautifully furnished seventeenth-century interior rather than for its exterior design.

ADDRESS
Les Huards, (M. Gendrier), Cour-Cheverny 41700 Contres.
A pleasant tasting cellar, with seemingly endless varieties of wines to try.

The growers in the town suffer from a surfeit of visitors to see the château, who wander in, try lots of wines and wander out again, having appreciated nothing and bought nothing. Let's try to put this situation to rights! It is something often mentioned to me, the main complaint being that this type of visitor doesn't show any *pleasure* in the grower's product, not that he doesn't buy any.

Many of the VDQS wines we have tasted recently have been very pleasant surprises indeed, and attractively priced; the Romorantin from a good year for instance has been compared favourably with a good Sancerre but is a fraction of the price. In this region you could also visit the Valençay vineyards, the Vendômois, the Orléanais and the Giennois.

CENTRAL LOIRE WINES

Everyone has heard of Sancerre and Pouilly-Fumé wines at the eastern end of the Loire Valley, but what about Quincy, Reuilly and Menetou-Salon? We made it our business recently to discover what goes on in these tiny regions and can recommend that anyone heading for Sancerre should select a route which takes him through those three places, starting with Reuilly.

REUILLY

How refreshing to find yourself pioneering new territory, as opposed to treading the well-worn paths in the wake of all the other tourists by the riverside. However, with pioneering come difficulties. Not having seen any sign of wine on offer at all in Reuilly except at a café, we resorted to our old trick of looking at a bottle label in a general shop, buying a bar of chocolate, then asking where that grower was to be found. It worked, and below are two places, since at the first, demand often outstrips supply, though the young grower is replanting as fast as he can. Growing vines needs patience however and he has to wait four years before his plants fruit.

ADDRESSES
Claude Lafond, Bois Saint-Denis, 36260 Reuilly.
Pleasant reception, we hope you are lucky!

Guy Malbete, Bois Saint-Denis, 36260 Reuilly. (Near the sports stadium).
Very friendly family. Full range of wines.

GRAPE VARIETIES
Sauvignon Blanc – dry white   Pinot Gris – rosé   Pinot Noir – red
The Pinot Gris is unique to Reuilly in qualifying as an AC wine, but it is the dry white of which it is most proud. This latter is very like Sancerre according to one grower, who hopes that if Sancerre's prices continue to be high, Reuilly might be able to compete favourably if it can expand its area.

QUINCY

Quincy, only a few kilometres from Reuilly, nevertheless produces an entirely different white wine, using the same Sauvignon grape. No need to buy chocolate here, venues are much easier to find, all with small notices.

ADDRESS
Domaine du Pressoir, (Claude Houssier), 18120 Quincy.
Lovely house and garden, friendly reception. Quincy only produces the one AC wine.
A visit to nearby medieval Bourges would combine perfectly with a wine tour of these little-frequented regions and it is here that you can learn about the historic events in which Jacques Coeur played such an important part. His name is used in many connections in this area, not all of them historic.

MENETOU-SALON

At the top of the enormous square at Menetou-Salon, you can find a large notice-board with the location and name of all the local growers, which is most helpful when arriving in a new area. A shop at the corner is run by the Vignerons de Jacques Coeur, the local union, where you can find out about the district and its history, but there is no need to buy there for private growers can be tracked down with persistence, using the giant map.

ADDRESS
Domaine de Chatanoy, Cave Clément, 18510 Menetou-Salon.
Friendly young grower. White, rosé and two reds, one aged in oak barrels for keeping five or six years.

Here the Pinot Noir is unique to the district for its red wine, and red accounts for two thirds of production at the above venue. Since Menetou-Salon shares the same grapes as its much more famous neighbour, it should be interesting to hasten on to Sancerre whilst the taste lingers and do a comparison!

SANCERRE AND POUILLY-FUMÉ

Here, the soil necessitates a change of grape and the Chenin Blanc is left behind as others take over to make the dry white wine this area has become famous for.

GRAPE VARIETIES
Sauvignon – for Sancerre and Pouilly-Fumé
Chasselas – for Pouilly-sur-Loire
Pinot Noir – for reds and rosés

It is obvious on entering the Sancerre district that finding a vineyard will be reasonably easy, for every village has its little signposts out. There are other things to distract the visitor however, which even share the wine-route signs here – goat cheeses, particularly around Chavignol. Vines sweep as far as the eye can see, relieved here and there by a field of goats, and Sancerre itself can be seen from a distance, commanding a view from all sides, since it is in the classical medieval *village perché* position. Buy your wine before visiting Sancerre is our advice – the town is riddled with wine and souvenir shops and its medieval aspect really rather spoilt by heavy commercialisation. The views from all sides make up for this, they are truly panoramic and well worth lingering over – a chunk of French bread, a *crottin de Chavignol*, and a glass of Sancerre to go with it makes a pleasant lunch stop on one of the strategically placed seats by the road up to the town.

ADDRESS
Clos du Chêne Marchand, (Lucien Crochet), Bué.
Not a family venue but pleasant reception. The red wine was a surprise since we had associated Sancerre with white. Our hostess remarked that it disappears very quickly, being very popular with the French themselves, whereas England is by far the largest importer of the white wine.

POUILLY

Pouilly offers two wines, the Pouilly-Fumé which is enjoying current popularity, and the Pouilly-sur-Loire which is not in the same class but is pleasant to drink whilst in the area, with a meal. St-Andelain is the direction to head for when looking for a vineyard for here the wines are reputed to be at their best. A *route du vin* is signed in these hills which incidentally seem to bear lots of fruit also.

This brings us to the end of the wine-producing part of this section of the Loire, though the river can be explored as far as the Rhône district for those who don't feel the need to taste wine all the way. The river itself is interesting in its own right throughout the region we have just covered; at times it can flood and create havoc, at times it is so dried up there are huge sand and gravel banks to walk on, and always there are opportunities for fishing (shad or *alose* is one of the local fish), water sports and just plain gazing into its reflections. Its smaller streams and tributaries ensure good growing land for fruits and vegetables, hence its 'garden of France' image, strawberries and asparagus being two of its main products which often feature together at local fairs.

We cannot leave this lovely area without a tail-piece. You might hear of it yourself in Tours, but in case you don't, you ought to know that the art of pruning was discovered by St Martin of Tours in AD345 with a little help from his donkey. The said animal was tied up to a post at the end of some vines and left to his own devices

Donzy le Pré, not far from Pouilly; delightful corners to explore

whilst the good St Martin went to give the monks in the fields the benefit of his wisdom concerning viticulture. The donkey became hungry and made a good meal of the young vine shoots and leaves before his master came back, for which he got a good ticking off, but instead of those particular branches bearing no fruit that year, they outstripped the others which had not been 'pruned', thus giving rise to the legend that this was where the method of cutting back was first discovered. Who can refute it?

LOCAL PRODUCTS AND SPECIALITIES
In this region, fresh fruits and vegetables must take first place, especially in Touraine.

Near the sea around Nantes, the local products are almost designed to marry with Muscadet wines and all along the river Loire, local fresh-water fish, notably pike *(brochet)*, is rendered delicious by a wine and butter sauce, *beurre blanc.*

Rillons and *rillettes* make good picnic fodder and of course the *crottins* of Sancerre are ideal too.

FURTHER INFORMATION
Western Loire: Comité Régional de Tourisme,
                Maison de Tourisme, Place du Commerce, F4400 Nantes.
Central Loire: Comité Régional de Tourisme,
                9, rue St Pierre Lentin, 45041 Orléans.

THE RHÔNE VALLEY

The Rhône is France's most powerful river, beginning its course high up in the St-Gotthard mountains in Switzerland, crashing through magnificent scenery as it descends in full spate, joining the Saône at Lyon and eventually emerging to flow across the plains of Provence into the Mediterranean near Marseille.

Wine was being made in the Rhône valley as early as the sixth century BC thanks to the trading instincts of the Greeks who, arriving at Marseille, wasted no time before exploring up-river, bringing their vine plants with them, the Syrah and the Viognier. The Romans continued the good work and got everyone organised with typical military precision into trading centres, and provided the roads and famous bridges which can still be witnessed today.

Not so long ago, the only Rhône wines of any account, as far as foreigners were concerned at least, were Châteauneuf-du-Pape and Hermitage, which have always enjoyed fame and prestige among wine lovers; the rest were considered cheap and cheerful, nothing else. Things have changed as you will not fail to notice if you sip your way slowly down the valley; people have banded together to alter the image and modern techniques have done the rest.

Since most tourists are heading south through this region on their way to the sea, that is the direction we shall take now, dividing the winelands into two parts, the north and the south, since they so conveniently do this for us geographically.

THE NORTHERN RHÔNE

This half of the region differs from the southern half in its granite base and its very steep slopes at either side of the river necessitating terracing and thus back- and leg-breaking work. Rain can wash down tons of surface soil which must be painstakingly replaced somehow in this area where very little use of machinery can be made. Little wonder that the wines of the three most northerly appellations are expensive, when one considers their small area of production and the unequal struggle which often goes into the growing of their vines.

CÔTE RÔTIE

This is the most northern vineyard of the Rhône, beginning just south of Vienne, and the oldest too, for it was here that the Greeks planted their Syrah and Viognier vines.

The very name Côte Rôtie, literally 'roasted slope' is itself evocative and derives from the fact that its steep terraces face direct south to catch the best of the sun. Some growers still divide it into *Blonde* and *Brune*, as can be seen from the rather ostentatious notices displayed among the vines; this custom dates back to the Middle Ages when a nobleman of Ampuis divided his land between his two daughters, one blonde, the other brunette.

GRAPE VARIETIES
Syrah
Viognier – just a small proportion added for fragrance
The wine is red, rich-coloured and strong and can be bought privately in Ampuis and Tupin.

CONDRIEU

Even less wine is produced for this appellation; it is a white wine, made uniquely from the Viognier, its rarity and high reputation unfortunately resulting in a high price also, but if you are looking for something 'different' here it is!

ADDRESS
Philippe Faury, La Ribaudry, Chavanay.
Our best, most secret vineyard, for which you need a head for heights! Condrieu supplies run out quickly, but St-Joseph is here too. Friendly family reception.

CHÂTEAU GRILLET

Within Condrieu, this wine is produced from the Viognier also, and made by the one château, its namesake. We daren't mention the price!

ST-JOSEPH

Coming down to something more accessible now, we can find the three wines of St-Joseph from as far north as Chavanay all the way down the N86 (which is the best route for discovering Rhône wine), until the Tournon area, where there is a concentration of vineyards. The route is often lovely, never far from the river, and any sortie into the hills will be rewarded by splendid long-distance views when the Rhône appears below like a silver ribbon. The wine St-Joseph is best known for is red, but white and rosé are also made. The vineyard used to be better known in the past and seems now to be making something of a comeback.

GRAPE VARIETIES
Syrah – Red

Rousanne }
Marsanne } White

St-Joseph red is a strong wine made for keeping for a few years whereas its white is to be enjoyed young. The white is often compared favourably with the white Hermitage across the river, but is considerably less expensive.

ADDRESS
See under Condrieu and Crozes-Hermitage.

HERMITAGE

Forsake not an old friend, for the new is not comparable to him; a new friend is as new wine, when it is old thou shalt drink it with pleasure.

ECCLESIASTICUS

To discover the renowned Hermitage and neighbouring Crozes-Hermitage, you need to cross the river to Tain, from which point you cannot possibly fail to see the most important thing around, the famous hill, swelling out behind the town in terraces, with the names of a certain two firms standing out as if proclaiming their stake in the goldmine. Although the vine was flourishing here since well before Christ, the name of the vineyard stems from the thirteenth century when a certain knight, Gaspard de Stérimberg arrived, from the crusades against the Albigensian heretics. It must have dawned on him that there was more to life than waving a sword around, for he retired from the fray to his '*érémitage*' here at Tain, where he exchanged his sword for a ploughshare in true biblical fashion and, when he was not meditating in solitude, he grew grapes.

The Hermitage red is what people usually call a 'big' or 'masculine' wine and needs keeping several years before it develops its full potential; the white has the versatility to be either enjoyed young or kept to develop. Do remember to check such points with your grower when selecting these wines however, for many growers are now producing wines which develop earlier and eliminate the storage difficulties which are always a problem for the non cellar-owning public.

FAMOUS VINEYARDS
La Chappelle – Red
Chante-Alouette – White

CROZES-HERMITAGE

Using the same grapes and growing them in a circle enclosing their prestigious neighbour, the Crozes-Hermitage *vignerons* offer similar wines at lower prices and it is therefore here that we would recommend the seeker of secret venues to wend his way. The wines need not be kept as long as the Hermitage before being ready which perhaps suits the modern way of life better.

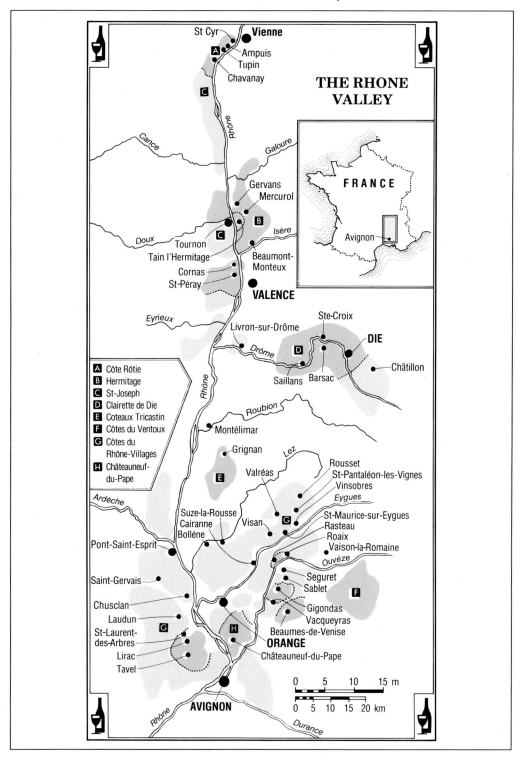

THE RHONE VALLEY

St Cyr · Vienne
Ampuis
Tupin
Chavanay

A Côte Rôtie

Gervans
Mercurol
Tournon
Tain l'Hermitage
Beaumont-Monteux
Cornas
St-Péray

VALENCE

Livron-sur-Drôme
Ste-Croix
DIE
Saillans · Barsac
Châtillon

Montélimar
Grignan
Valréas
Rousset
St-Pantaléon-les-Vignes
Vinsobres
Suze-la-Rousse
Cairanne
Bollène
Visan
St-Maurice-sur-Eygues
Rasteau
Roaix
Vaison-la-Romaine
Pont-Saint-Esprit
Saint-Gervais
Seguret
Sablet
Chusclan
Laudun
Gigondas
Vacqueyras
St-Laurent-des-Arbres
Beaumes-de-Venise
Lirac
ORANGE
Tavel
Châteauneuf-du-Pape

AVIGNON

FRANCE
Avignon

A	Côte Rôtie
B	Hermitage
C	St-Joseph
D	Clairette de Die
E	Coteaux Tricastin
F	Côtes du Ventoux
G	Côtes du Rhône-Villages
H	Châteauneuf-du-Pape

0   5   10   15 m
0   5   10   15   20 km

Don't buy your Crozes-Hermitage in Tain itself, head for the villages on our map. Even if one or two of your sorties up the narrow lanes might be abortive, as our recent ones were, you gain height very quickly and are rewarded with magnificent panoramic views over the Rhône valley, particularly from those hills north of Tain.

ADDRESS
Domaine la Négociale, (Collonge), Mercurol.
In the process of expansion, M. Collonge offers a good example of a man moving with the times, yet keeping the family image. A wide selection of wines and the facility for coping with groups.

CORNAS AND ST-PÉRAY

These two vineyards are so close to each other that one tasting venue will most likely suffice for trying them both, but they are totally different wines.

Cornas is made solely of Syrah grapes and the wine is known for its very dark colour and its powers of ageing. It certainly needs to be kept several years before its true characteristics are displayed.

St-Péray specialises in a sparkling wine, for its particular position and soils give an aspect to its wine which lends itself perfectly to the Champagne method. Like Cornas, it is only a small vineyard and its produce is most easily found in the Verilhac cellars in St-Péray itself. For an eagle's eye view over the Rhône, visit the ruins of the Château de Crussol.

Before leaving the northern Côtes du Rhône, and munching your way through the miles of fruit-growing land between the two Côtes, there is one more journey to make if you don't want to pass by anything untried. A word of warning however, for this journey leads you into such a beautiful countryside that it could well be that your plans for travelling further south may have to be delayed a few days, or even put off until another year. Such is the scenery and atmosphere to be found by following the river Drôme into the Parc du Vercors and beyond.

CLAIRETTE DE DIE

Clairette de Die was already appreciated by the early Romans before we tourists arrived on the scene and is a golden-coloured sparkling wine of which the local people are very proud. It can be made by the Champagne method but very often the traditional method is preferred which was always used from time immemorial before 'new-fangled ideas' came into this part of the world. By the natural method, the half-fermented wine, rich in its grape sugar, is put into bottles with nothing added, and allowed to finish its fermentation slowly, thus keeping the flavour and aroma of the Muscat grape.

GRAPE VARIETIES
Muscat
Clairette

ADDRESS
Vincent Achard, Ste-Croix.
A lovely old ramshackle building by the river, chickens running loose, vines surrounding it. Family welcome.

Here we met the son of the property, an absolute enthusiast for 'nature and progress' as shown on his signboard. Chemicals are used on the vines as little as possible and everything is done traditionally, letting nature take its course. The young man was almost as effervescent as his wines when expounding his theories but had a genuine concern for the consumer, who, he says, is receiving far too much sulphur dioxide in the wines he buys from less concerned growers. You have been warned!

A further wine region is reached as you are lured toward the hills, that of Châtillon-en-Diois, giving light reds and whites, suitable for enjoying on the spot.

THE SOUTHERN CÔTES DU RHÔNE

The geography and climate of this region differ completely from that of the north. Firstly, the banks of the river flatten so that vines are no longer perching on steep terraces and the area covered width-ways is nearly as much as that which runs north/south. Secondly, the sun beats down more fiercely in summer and for a longer period, and the Mistral wind blows directly down the valley. You will notice from here onwards the presence of tall reeds which are grown specifically to be made into anti-Mistral devices around homes and produce, as well as the many living hedges of cypress trees and the artificial protections erected in the nurseries. The rolling nature of the countryside permits far more production than the difficult north since there is room for planting and suitable terrain for mechanisation, therefore prices too tend to be lower for the general appellation Rhône wine. A further difference is in the retailing of the wines, for the south makes much more use than the north of co-operatives. Finally, grape varieties in the south abound whereas the north abides by just one or two.

CÔTES DU RHÔNE

This is the general appellation for Rhône wine, the bulk of it being made in the southern côtes. These wines will vary according to the kind of land they are grown on and according to the use the *vigneron* makes of his different vines, for there are many to choose from. Currently very popular is the Rhône's answer to the Beaujolais, its *primeur* wine, which appears on exactly the same date, November 15th.

GRAPE VARIETIES

The Rhône growers are spoilt for choice but below are the main ones:

Red: Grenache (the principal one), Syrah, Mourvèdre, Cinsaut, Carignan
White: Clairette, Bourboulenc

The first vineyard you will meet as you head southwards through the delicious fruit region is the Coteaux de Tricastin on the left bank of the river.

COTEAUX DE TRICASTIN

This vineyard like many others of France used to be far more vigorous until phylloxera wiped it out in the 1890s. It is now back in business making red and a little rosé and is experimenting with grape varieties not normally used in this area. No doubt the proximity of the university of wine at Suze-la-Rousse, formerly a medieval château, has something to do with this. Also in the Tricastin are two-thirds of France's truffle supply, so here is added reason to call in on your way south. Traditionally pigs were used to sniff out these rare and expensive delicacies from under the oak trees, but it has now been found more convenient to use dogs. Did you know that a good dog can find two or three kilogrammes of truffles per hour?

CÔTES DU RHÔNE-VILLAGES

In the same way that Beaujolais and the Roussillon, for example, have allowed several communes to add their names to the general appellation, so have seventeen communes been granted the right here in the Rhône, each being deemed to have recognisable qualities in its wines. Most are red, with the exception being Laudun and Chusclan, Laudun making white and Chusclan rosé. A vividly painted notice board will announce for you the name of the wine region as you enter it – there is no hiding of lights under bushels down here! The bulk of the Côtes du Rhône-Villages wines are to be found in the beautiful Vaucluse area, which is simply crying out to be explored, that is, as far as the Dentelles de Montmirail will permit. Once you begin your foray into the *arrière-pays* out here, it is easy to forget about the more famous wines behind you and concentrate on discovering one secret vineyard after another, particularly if you stay clear of the bigger towns.

RASTEAU AND BEAUMES DE VENISE

A visit to either of these two is useful for it combines several styles of wine, including of course the *vin doux naturel* (see p.133) found only in the south of France. Beaumes de Venise is the better known VDN, made entirely of the Muscat grape whereas Rasteau uses the Grenache. The former is drunk young to capture its muscat flavour and aroma, but Rasteau can be left for a while to develop.

Typical Côtes du Rhône-Villages country in the Vaucluse district

ADDRESS
Domaine la Soumade, (André Romero), Rasteau 84110 Vaison-la-Romaine.
Here is the Rasteau VDN expert. He also offers Côtes du Rhône and Côtes du Rhône-Villages Rasteau, so the visitor can make some comparisons between these last two.

GIGONDAS

Gigondas has been granted its own appellation, having risen rapidly through the ranks, and is a powerful red wine, made for keeping several years. The name Gigondas has an interesting origin for it comes directly from *jocunditas*, the Latin for joy, and since it was the Romans themselves who founded the vineyard in the century before Christ, it seems that they chose the name deliberately, in view of the great pleasure the produce of this special situation was giving them. The pleasure for the tourist is not only in the wine, for the little town itself nestles at the foot of the Dentelles de Montmirail, surrounded by medieval ramparts, with a very interesting fifth-century chapel crowning it. All this and the mountains for a backdrop could put a lesser wine into second place!

ADDRESS
Domaine de Raspail-Ay, (Dominique Ay), Gigondas.

Here the emphasis is on a natural product; all work is done manually and traditionally. Family firm.

CÔTES DU VENTOUX

The Côtes du Ventoux is also in the beautiful Vaucluse region and offers the visitor three different wine routes for discovering not only its wines but the historically interesting countryside too, all routes starting at Carpentras.

Lovers of Roman history must make sure they have visited Orange, Carpentras and Vaison-la-Romaine before leaving this fascinating area to discover why Châteauneuf-du-Pape is so well known.

CHÂTEAUNEUF DU PAPE

Before talking about this wine, we ought to look first to nearby Avignon and its history which will explain the name of Châteauneuf-du-Pape. In 1305 the Archbishop of Bordeaux was crowned Pope through some manoeuvrings of Philip IV of France, and he moved to Avignon complete with his title of Clement V and his entourage. There the Papacy remained for sixty-eight years, closely guarded inside the Palais des Papes, one of the world's biggest feudal castles. One of the Popes, becoming bored with this environment, built a summer residence a few miles further north, the 'new castle of the Pope', as today's name literally translates. As ever, the Church knew how to get the best out of a grape-vine and that was the beginning of what is now one of the Rhône's most well-known wines all over the world. Only a fraction of the castle remains today as a reminder, but the acres of vines are there for all to see.

One of the most surprising things to learn about Châteauneuf-du-Pape is that it can be made up from any of thirteen grape varieties. It is usually thought that a predominance of one variety gives that wine its character. Not so here! The growers will all be able to reel off for you which grape gives which characteristic and it will be their own idea of proportions in the blending which marks the difference between one château's wine and another's.

The red wines are sometimes made lighter and ready for quicker drinking than they used to be in the days when you didn't open the bottle for at least ten years. However, they have retained their high alcohol content, the highest in France, and their deep colour.

Conditions in the vineyard contribute to this alcoholic content for in addition to growing under very hot sun all summer and autumn, the huge white stones, which you cannot fail to notice in this area, retain that heat after the sun has faded, and reflect it back up to the vines, which furthers the ripening of the grapes.

Châteauneuf itself is gaudy with signs for *vente directe* which do not make for pleasant searching at all and we would recommend you look in one of the neighbouring communes instead, for there is plenty of choice. Courthézon,

Bedarrides and Sorgues will all have the wine for sale. Here at Châteauneuf there are real châteaux as opposed to small plots and co-operatives: Chateau Fortia; Domaine de Mont-Redon; Domaine des Fines Roches.

ADDRESS
Domaine de Nalys, Route de Courthézon, 84230 Châteauneuf-du-Pape.
Large and well known, but outside the town and pleasant to visit. Try their white too, it is highly rated. White tends to be forgotten in this red area and might bring you some surprises.

LIRAC AND TAVEL

Tavel makes rosé wines only and has achieved a considerable reputation for them, but on looking at its close neighbour Lirac, we decided without any hesitation to do our rosé tasting there, for Tavel is too geared up for tourists to put it bluntly, and has no charm about it whatsoever compared with nearby Lirac and its villages, which not only make rosé on the same terrain with the same grape as Tavel, but offer a red and white into the bargain.

St-Laurent-des-Arbes, one of Lirac's villages, is a truly delightful little cluster of white stone buildings culminating in the picturesque church overlooking it all, and furthermore, has a fully operational *lavoir*, where the local women beat out their washing in much the same way as their ancestors did centuries ago, except for the use of washing powder!

ADDRESS
Domaine Rousseau, (M. Rousseau), Les Charmettes, 30290 Laudun.
A most interesting proprietor, excellent English spoken, and three wines offered. Very cordial welcome.

LOCAL PRODUCTS AND SPECIALITIES
The Rhône tends to be influenced by the gastronomic centre of Lyon, but has a few of its own specialities too.
Grives and *alouettes* – thrushes and larks are unfortunately made into pâtés here.
Nougat comes from Montélimar.
Fruits of every variety are noted in the Rhône, also early vegetables. Provençal food, making much use of olive oil and herbs, is found in the south.

FURTHER INFORMATION
Comité Régional du Tourisme,
5 Place de la Baleine,
69005 Lyon

THE
SOUTHWEST

The Southwest is a vague geographical term in use to denote the regions outlined below whose wines and terrains bear little relationship to each other, except that they all lie in the southwest of France. Bordeaux is of course also in this geographical area, but as a wine region is deemed worthy of its own title. One wine writer lumps all the southwest wines under the undistinguished title of 'lesser wines of France'; I would like to alter this to 'lesser-*known* wines of France' and in the following pages will try to convey some of the atmosphere of the southwest vineyards, for exciting things are happening beyond the borders of Bordeaux.

Many of the wines of this broad area have suffered and still suffer to some extent from the presence of Bordeaux, so near and so well known. Remember however, that in the not so distant past, when the Bordeaux wines were rather light it was the strong wines of Cahors and Fronton to name just two, which the merchants had sent up to them by canal or river, to 'doctor' their own weak brew in certain years. The mechanisms by the canalside at Fronton can still be seen today whereby the barrels were loaded on to barges to be taken straight to Bordeaux. Not only were their wines used to strengthen Bordeaux ones, these southwestern producers were often treated rather like vassals by their powerful neighbour, who of course had the backing of the English and a very strategic position as major port. They were, in other words, swallowed up by Bordeaux merchants and only recently have been able to stand on their own feet and assert their own individual character.

Character is the keyword for all these appellations and it is the character of the unusual and often ancient local grape varieties, coupled with that of the highly individual growers, each proud of his own particular heritage, which together produce the intriguing selection of wine styles on offer in this area.

If this is not enough to whet the appetite of the inquisitive wine lover, consider some of the regions in which they are produced – the Tarn, the Dordogne, the foothills of the Pyrenees; all of them scenically beautiful, historically interesting, or both. There is one more aspect to mention about all these wines and that is their excellent value for money, for in view of the fact that they are still, many of them, building or re-building their reputations, their growers have enough to do with improving the quality of their wines leaving little time or money for advertising or

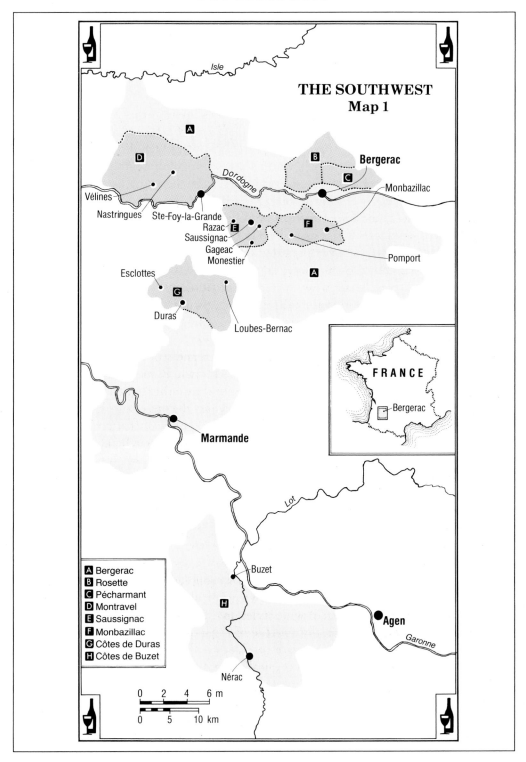

THE SOUTHWEST
Map 1

Isle

A

D

Vélines

Nastringues

Ste-Foy-la-Grande

B

Bergerac

C

Dordogne

Monbazillac

Razac

E

Saussignac

Gageac

Monestier

F

Pomport

A

Esclottes

G

Duras

Loubes-Bernac

FRANCE

Bergerac

Marmande

Lot

Buzet

H

Agen

Garonne

Nérac

A Bergerac
B Rosette
C Pécharmant
D Montravel
E Saussignac
F Monbazillac
G Côtes de Duras
H Côtes de Buzet

0   2   4   6 m

0   5   10 km

high-powered sales techniques, thus they are not widely recognised enough to command the price they might. Watch out for them in the future and pay a visit now is our advice!

BERGERAC

Bergerac city itself has been at the centre of French-English disputes for centuries, ending with the Hundred Years War in the mid-thirteenth century when it was returned to France forever. These wars have left the area well populated with the castles and forts which cannot help but feature on your photographs of riverside scenery, and which attract thousands of visitors throughout the summer months. There have been other wars however, not so well documented: only after three centuries of struggles and bitter disputes with big brother Bordeaux did the wine of Bergerac win the right to circulate freely all the year round in the Dordogne in 1520. Today you will have no problem in finding something to your taste, from the general Bergerac appellation through to the remotest outpost of Saussignac.

BERGERAC, CÔTES DE BERGERAC

Under these two names can be found reds, whites and rosés, the white varying from dry to the sweet *moelleux*. The Côtes de Bergerac label will denote that its reds will have more body than those of the plain Bergerac label and in the case of white wine, the Côtes will be sweeter.

ADDRESS
Domaine du Grand Vignal, (Jean Pierre Roulet), Repenty, Monestier.
The unassuming young grower here wins prizes for nearly all the above categories, particularly *sec* and *moelleux*. Deep in the countryside, a challenge to locate!

GRAPE VARIETIES
The same as in Bordeaux:

Cabernet Sauvignon
Cabernet Franc } Red
Merlot
Malbec

Sauvignon
Sémillon } White
Muscadelle

Not far from Monestier lies the sleepy village of Saussignac; a visit to the two could be combined, using the *route des vins* provided.

SAUSSIGNAC

The Saussignac sweet wine is said by many to take its place between the Côtes de Bergerac *moelleux* and the Monbazillac *liquoreux* wines – the only way to test this opinion is to go there and find out for yourself.

ADDRESS
Château Court les Muts, (P. Sadoux), Razac de Saussignac 24240 Sigoulès.
Delightfully situated deep in the country. Tasting in the *chais*. English spoken. A visit round the property is offered and a full range of Bergerac wines is made, Saussignac a speciality.

Although Saussignac wine is probably unheard of apart from in Bergerac, it has been going strong since the fourteenth century and is made according to the traditional methods used at Sauternes (see p.23) and neighouring Monbazillac, relying on the Sémillon grapes in particular and the *pourriture noble* brought on by early morning mists and sunny afternoons. To compare the three local sweet wines, why not include a visit to Monbazillac during the one tour whilst the memory of each is fresh?

MONBAZILLAC

Monbazillac is of course the better-known sweet white wine of this region, at one time considered a rival to the great Sauternes. After the Second World War, everyone seemed to want this style of wine, resulting in too much being produced and the quality level falling as a direct consequence. Now however, the future is brighter for the sweet wine producers, for vinification is much better (less sulphur dioxide, no more headaches), and restrictions have been placed on production, thus protecting the good name of all the conscientious growers. Both Saussignac and Monbazillac break all rules by coming from vines grown on northern slopes. The imposing Château Monbazillac, perched on a knoll overlooking a peaceful panorama is impressive to look at but is now a co-operative. There are plenty of private growers to visit.

ADDRESS
Château Charrut, (Charles Charrut), Malveyrein, Pomport.
It is a pleasure to find this rural corner of Bergerac. Monbazillac here is highly rated by neighbouring vineyard owners, always a good sign.

Both these last two wines need time in the bottle to reach their full potential; as with Sauternes, you must be patient, though it must be confessed, they taste delicious to me even when young.

We go now across the Dordogne to locate the three other areas which come under the Bergerac banner, beginning with the two nearest to Bergerac itself.

PÉCHARMANT

Here Bergerac's longest-keeping red wine is produced, on the slopes immediately surrounding the town, deriving its particular taste from the iron in its gravelly soil. A *route des vins* guides the visitor through the vineyards to locate the growers but initially it might be difficult to find a road directly into the region; a small sign 'Pécharmant' will lead you up out of the eastern end of the town. The wine will be difficult for the novice to taste, for it doesn't 'open up' for three years and reaches its fullness between five and seven; the growers are anxious for newcomers to appreciate this factor when tasting.

ADDRESS
Domaine du Haut Pécharmant, (Mme. Reine Roches),
Pécharmant 24100 Bergerac.
A warm welcome here and a product made without chemicals. Doctors have voted in its favour. Mother is in charge of operations, domaine in the family for centuries. Watch for the '85 Veuve Reine released shortly!

A short trip through the back roads will take you to the neighbouring Rosette vineyard where you can track down one of the five growers of this little-known wine.

ROSETTE

The history behind Rosette's vineyard reveals that once it was much larger, but the powers that be, the new burghers of Bergerac, decreed that all vines should be grown on the other side of the river to be recognised as good wine; the vineyard of Rosette sadly dwindled therefore until just recently when one owner decided that he would make it his aim to put Rosette wine back on the map. It is a sweet white wine, 'somewhere in the middle between Monbazillac and Bergerac *moelleux,*' to quote the grower himself, yet preserving its own unique flavour gained from its terrain and position.

ADDRESS
Château Puypezat, (Bernard frères), Rosette 24100 Bergerac.
The young grower is concerned that this appellation should be more widely known. Friendly welcome in rural surroundings.

The Rosette wine is overshadowed by the name and fame of Monbazillac even though its wine is nothing like it. Growers are waiting for the day when people wake up and realise that all local sweet wine is not Monbazillac. Here is your opportunity to test out the differences for yourself and take note of the price differences too.

MONTRAVEL

The Montravel region follows on naturally from the Castillon region of Bordeaux; it is easy to see how Bergerac wine was absorbed by Bordeaux until it began fighting for

Castles and forts cannot help but feature in your photographs of Dordogne riverside scenery – here is Belcastel

its own identity. Montravel specialises in white wines, producing a dry one and two levels of sweet, Haut-Montravel and Côtes de Montravel. It is only a small region but plenty of growers are waiting to show us their wines. They are a close community and have prepared information and addresses for the tourist.

ADDRESS
Domaine de Libarde, (J. C. Banizette), Nastringues 24230 Vélines.
A farmhouse-style welcome, full range of wines and very attractive prices.

All the wines of Bergerac seem to be made to match up to the celebrated Périgord cuisine and as if to prove this harmony, the farmers and *vignerons* have produced a booklet which sets out canton by canton where the various farm products can be located, who is offering farmhouse accommodation and so on. The booklet is free, found at all the welcoming venues of this hospitable Bergerac region.

Many venues will have a full range of other Bergerac appellation wines apart from the one their area specialises in, so don't be surprised to be confronted with an array of different labels at times. A word of advice however; if you want to go through the lot, be prepared to make a reasonable purchase, it is only fair after using up the grower's valuable time.

CÔTES DE DURAS

This vineyard can be included in a Bordeaux or a Bergerac tour, since it borders both. It is a classical example of the determination of a number of *vignerons* to resuscitate a once-vigorous vineyard laid low by wars and phylloxera. The last thirty years have seen enormous activity and replanting and have given birth in particular to a white, fruity Sauvignon wine gaining rapidly in popularity. Sweet white, red and rosé are also made. The red wines will be found either ready to drink or to keep, according to which methods the *vigneron* has used when making them. A recently organised *route des vins* will take you through the main producing areas, where you can find a large number of private growers to choose from.

ADDRESS
Domaine de Laulan, (Gilbert Geoffrey), Laulan 47120 Duras.
Directions for this address can be found at the Château de Duras information bureau. A friendly welcome; yet another man passionately enjoying his work. White Sauvignon a speciality.

We especially remember M. Geoffrey for the sheer excitement and pleasure he displayed on opening one of his '82 red wines and discovering that for the first time he could smell vanilla! He simply could not keep quiet about it, it was a wonderful moment for him to realise that the product he had been working on was actually developing the way he had hoped. Though outwardly an undemonstrative man, he described wine as a poem, a work of art, just as another grower not far away had compared the making of wine with creating a picture. The harvest, the latter said, comes to hand as always, and yes, the *vigneron* has equipment in his *chai* and certain knowledge inside himself, but he has before him at that time an empty canvas upon which to paint the picture.

These kind of remarks are simply not heard at the larger domaines or at co-operatives where men pool their harvest and knowledge.

CÔTES DE BUZET

Lest it be thought that we haven't a kind word for co-operatives, we shall now go on to describe the activities of one in particular, thanks to which the whole vineyard of the Côtes de Buzet has been revived after its phylloxera sufferings. The reader will have realised that in some areas growers could not survive without the co-operatives' facilities. Sometimes the wine produced at the co-operatives is even better made than that of some private growers, as blind tastings have proved. However, there is no substitute for the enthusiast who is dying to have his product appreciated, is proud of his heritage and loves meeting new people, and it is here that the visit to the co-operative can disappoint.

ADDRESS
Les Vignerons Réunis des Côtes de Buzet, Buzet sur Baïse, 47160 Damazon.
Factory-like exterior but pleasant modern tasting room. Well-informed, helpful
staff. A visit to the cooper's yard if you are lucky.

The Côtes de Buzet, an almost entirely red region, is yet another of the vineyards
which suffered from the 'Bordeaux syndrome' in that the *Privilège des Vins de
Bordeaux* gave Bordeaux the sole trading rights with northern Europe. Buzet had no
option but to be swallowed up by its powerful neighbour, even though it had the
small satisfaction of supplying strong wine for 'doctoring' purposes. The Bordeaux
privilege was abolished in 1776 but the after-effects lingered. In 1911 Bordeaux
placed stricter limits on its area, Buzet was excluded, and had to look to finding its
own markets; on top of phylloxera it was almost too much and there was more to
come in the shape of two wars. However, the wine advanced to VDQS status, with
more care taken over planting the 'noble' grape varieties, and after the formation of
the co-operative in 1955 things shot ahead. This union of like-minded men put
everything into better production and better salesmanship with the result that AC
status was gained and they now aim confidently at the top.

GRAPE VARIETIES
As for Bordeaux.
One of Buzet's secrets must lie in the ageing in oak barrels, made by their own
resident cooper; if you get the opportunity, ask to see the 4,000 barrels in the vast
cellar.

If you are visiting the Buzet cellars, you should not miss the chance to look around
Nérac nearby, with its Henry IV interest and the lovely old medieval part of the town
down by the river. You cannot fail too to see how much plum brandy there is on offer
as you tour the region, nor what a prolific fruit and vegetable garden this is. Tomatoes
become much in evidence further north, leading to Marmande which is famous for
both these and its VDQS wine.

CÔTES DU MARMANDAIS

Both red and white wines are produced and some intriguing grape varieties are added
to the Bordeaux mix in the shape of Abouriou, Bovillet, and Grappu. The result of all
that can be tasted at the Buzet co-op if you don't manage to reach those at Marmande.

CAHORS

Cahors is the next southwest region to discover, possibly the most well known of
them all and proud of its Roman past. If you are combining wine-visits with all the
other delights of this diversified region, there is one particular route which ought to

be followed to connect Bergerac with Cahors or of course vice-versa. Admittedly it is not the most direct but it allows you to explore the Dordogne and the Lot valleys, to say nothing of the Célé, tributary of the Lot. So much happens along this route that only another book could justify its telling but here we shall just mention the many famous prehistoric caves of Quercy, the fairytale settlements of Rocamadour and St-Cirq-Lapopie, the castles, and the sheer grandeur of much of the scenery, to say nothing of the ancient shepherd huts on the Causses and the *cabécous* cheeses up there. (For details of this route see the end of the chapter.) Back now to wine, which happily unites the two valleys, Dordogne and Lot, though wine of a different nature entirely in Cahors.

Cahors is used to fame and doesn't hesitate to tell us how it was once used to 'top

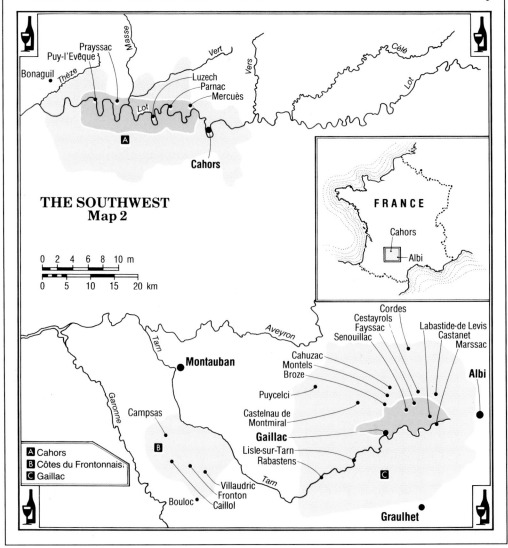

St-Cirq-Lapopie on the Lot, fairytale settlement

up' Bordeaux and how its growers were summoned to Châteauneuf to give the Pope the benefit of their viticultural wisdom.

GRAPE VARIETIES
Cot Noir or Malbec (local name Auxerrois) – principal variety
Merlot
Tannat
The wine is deep red and powerful, capable of ageing well, but now made by many growers to be pleasant when young too. At one time, Cahors was scarcely palatable for its first dozen or so years and had a colour verging on black. A wine route connects the important areas of production and spectacular sights such as the castle at Bonaguil and the Pont Valentré at Cahors itself keep the tourist on the move.

ADDRESS
Domaine de Fantou, Juillac, near Preyssac.
A young husband and wife team here, and an old family property. Friendly and enthusiastic welcome. A selection of Cahors available, ready to drink or to keep.
It was whilst visiting this well-kept venue by the riverside that we met a sprightly eighty-two year old, looking about sixty, having his cannister filled up ready for the next few days' consumption. His bottle a day, he reckoned, was the secret of his good

health and happiness, and we discovered that the young couple also drank a bottle at midday and actually managed to work hard for the rest of the afternoon in the vines or *chai*. Many of the outdoor workers have their bottle with them for the lunch-break, a modern version of the tiny barrel which used to be carried for the same purpose, and we couldn't help but wonder what chaos might ensue if we developed this habit in England?

It is to a little-known region that we turn now, that of Gaillac on the Tarn, whose vineyard is strategically placed for us to combine a visit with the discovery of Albi and the fabulous Gorges du Tarn further upstream.

GAILLAC

Gaillac appears to offer us everything for it boasts several different terrains, each particularly suited to some of the many different and mostly unusual grape varieties.

GRAPE VARIETIES

Mauzac			Gamay	
l'En de l'El			Duras	
Muscadelle	} White		Négrette	} Red
Sauvignon			Syrah	
Ondenc			And others...	

If Gaillac is little known now it was not always so, for it used to be famous for its sweet white wine of the Premières Côtes. This wine is still being made with the Mauzac, one of the local grapes, but there is also a dry white, a red and a *mousseux*. Plenty of growers offer their produce for sale but we think there can be none quite so passionately interested in the vine and its product as the one we were fortunate to meet recently, Robert Plageoles.

ADDRESS
Domaine Roucou-Cantemerle, (Robert Plageoles),
81140 Castelnau de Montmiral.
Family vineyard since the 1400s. Whole range of Gaillac made, plus 'extras' unique to this *vigneron*. A visit is an education.

Here at this vineyard work is going on to revive a long-forgotten vine, the Ondenc, not used in wine-making for a century. The vision of a father, the patient research of a son, and that son's determination to let nature rule and produce the grapes it always did on this land will one day make the rest of the world's sweet wine producers sit up and take notice. What is special about the Ondenc here? Suffice it to say that in the Middle Ages there were '*gardes de vignes*' who kept watch day and night to make sure that no-one stole from this vineyard, and anyone caught was dealt with very severely.

There is an exciting air of mystery about this project, and we only hope we are around to taste the first fruits.

It is not our intention to dwell on the dreams or achievements of any one grower, but it must be said that Robert Plageoles, though more exuberant and eloquent than most, is typical of so many others in this southwest region where so much personality both of growers and of vines is found. They respect the vine as a living, intelligent being almost, and work side by side with it rather than trying to master it. Many of the southwest growers are keen on using new oak barrels in their vinification process now, which, they claim, adds a certain 'something' to the red wines in particular. The barrels are renewed every three or four years, an expensive process which is nevertheless not reflected in the price of their wines to the consumer. These men look on vine-dressing primarily as a way of life, not a commercial proposition, a refreshing attitude which has struck us on our travels through all the lesser-known regions recently.

Not far from Gaillac, another interesting little region can be located, just north of Toulouse, the Côtes du Frontonnais.

CÔTES DU FRONTONNAIS

This region makes red and rosé wines, Fronton and Villaudric being able to add their names to the label. The originality of Fronton wine lies not surprisingly in its main grape variety used.

GRAPE VARIETIES
Négrette, principally
Gamay
Syrah
Cabernet Franc and Sauvignon
The Négrette is difficult to work on, both outside and in the *chai*, but the Fronton growers persist doggedly, knowing that they have a unique characteristic in their wine. Both rosé and red are to be drunk young, the latter being able to age if so desired, but an interesting remark was made by our grower on this subject: he has noticed that many people think that they must keep a wine as long as possible for it to be 'good'; this simply is not so he says, except for a few classics such as are produced in Bordeaux.

Wine is readily available in this small area and a *route des vins* is currently being planned.

ADDRESS
Domaine de Joliet, (François Daubert),Caillol, 31620 Fronton.
A young husband and wife team, but a very old property. Both are happy to meet visitors and explain everything.

THE FAR SOUTH AND WEST

The third group into which this southwest region falls is the most southern and western, containing a varied selection of little-known wines, many of them made with local grape varieties not in use anywhere else in France. Travellers passing through on their way to Spain or the Pyrenees via the coastal route, or indeed those visiting Lourdes must make time to break the journey and turn off the motorway, for all of the following wines are easily reached.

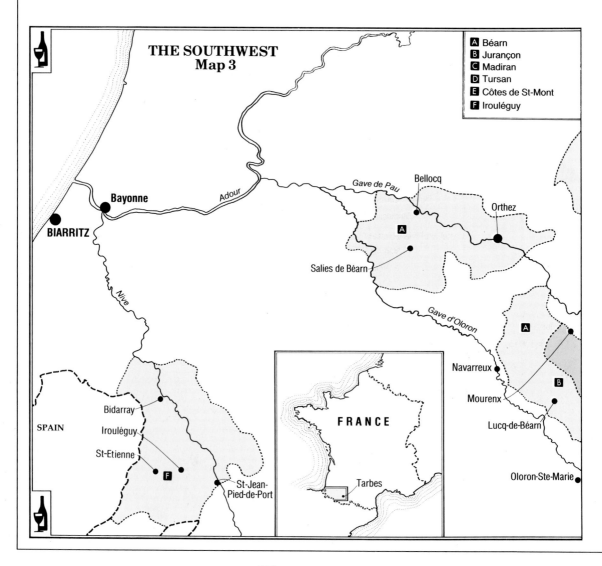

**THE SOUTHWEST
Map 3**

A Béarn
B Jurançon
C Madiran
D Tursan
E Côtes de St-Mont
F Irouléguy

Gave de Pau
Bellocq
Orthez
Bayonne
Adour
BIARRITZ
A
Salies de Béarn
Gave d'Oloron
Nive
Navarreux
Mourenx
B
Lucq-de-Béarn
Bidarray
Irouléguy
St-Etienne
SPAIN
F
St-Jean-
Pied-de-Port
FRANCE
Tarbes
Oloron-Ste-Marie

CÔTES DE BÉARN

Béarn is best known for its rosé though red is also made, and can be found in the Orthez and Salies de Béarn district as well as in the two areas for Madiran and Jurançon. At Orthez there is the thirteenth-century fortified bridge to see, and Salies de Béarn provides the salt from its mines for the curing of the famous Bayonne hams of the area. Two individual wines within the general Béarn appellation could not be more unalike – Jurançon and Madiran.

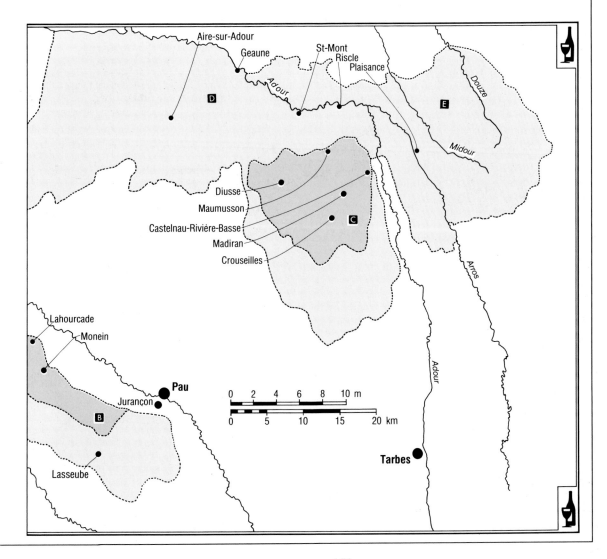

JURANÇON

Jurançon and Madiran growers were two of the south-west's number who were able to sell their own wine, using Bayonne as their exporting outlet, whilst their fellow growers nearer Bordeaux suffered in serfdom, unable to sell under their own name.

The Jurançon wine is all white and its growers like to claim fame by telling us that Good King Henry IV was christened with it, having a few drops passed over his lips as soon as he was born. Good King Henry's name has appeared nearly all over France in connection with regional wines so the Jurançon's growers probably have something to answer for, starting him off so young!

The sweetest wine is the one which has always been associated with Jurançon, but there is a dry one also gaining in popularity, for some of the growers find that it is too risky a business waiting often into November before the grapes for the sweet wine reach their overripe stage and can be picked. You will see photographs of harvesting scenes in the snow as you tour the cellars, and the older growers in particular will tell you how the vineyard has shrunk not only since phylloxera but since the advent of the motor car, which enabled the young men to go and find work in the towns as opposed to in the vines in the days when there was usually no option but to follow in father's footsteps. Grassed-over terraces on the slopes of the foothills all around Pau witness to this fact. Vines are noticeably higher than elsewhere, to avoid the spring frosts in this region and grape varieties are ancient.

GRAPE VARIETIES
Petit Manseng ⎫
Gros Manseng ⎬ Mainly
Courbu ⎭

Mixed farming is practised here, with vineyards literally hiding away, but always on the best sunniest slopes in pretty, undulating countryside when you finally track them down.

ADDRESS
Clos-Uroulat, (Charles Hours), 64360 Monein.
A young oenologist works this property, having given up teaching wine students at Bordeaux to apply his skills to his own patch. Jurançon *sec*, *moelleux* and a red Béarn are made.

Owing to the fact that the sweet wine is kept an unusually long time in the barrel before bottling, and in view of the difficulties of harvesting, the *moelleux* is not as easily found as the *sec* which represents less costs, but this countryside is offering other products in the form of local ewes' milk cheeses, so at least the journey can have a two-fold reason behind it, to make it more worthwhile.

MADIRAN

Here, not far away, is the exact opposite of Jurançon. Madiran is dark red, often unpalatable for its first few years but able to develop in both flavour and bouquet as the years pass. There is however another red Madiran which is designed to give you a highly individual wine still, yet one which can be enjoyed young. The local grape variety accounts for this individuality.

GRAPE VARIETIES
Tannat
Cabernet Franc and Sauvignon, plus the Fer Savadou
The Tannat sets this wine apart as being truly regional, the higher the proportion being used, the more 'virile' the resulting wine. The Madiran vineyards have an interesting connection with Burgundy, for it was the Cistercian monks who brought their local vines with them and set up the Madiran vineyards just before founding the famous Clos de Vougeot. The vineyard, diminished through phylloxera but awarded its AC in 1948, was taken in hand by a new generation of growers, with new ideas but the same aim in mind, that of keeping their regional wine alive and bringing it to the world's notice. One of their leading lights single-mindedly pursues this object from the estate below.

ADDRESS
Chateau Montus, (Alain Brumont),
Domaine du Bouscassé, Maumusson 32400 Riscle.
Prize-winning wines here, Madiran, Pacherenc and Béarn rosé. Ageing in new oak casks. Efficient reception.

PACHERENC DU VIC BIHL

The very name has intrigued me ever since I came across it, and in view of the legendary rarity of its sweet as opposed to its dry white wine, we determined this year to find it. Most of the Madiran growers have Pacherenc, but it is not always the *moelleux*. One of the Vic Bihl grape varieties is exclusively used just there, the Arrufiat, and is the one being used for replanting, thus testifying once more to the desire of so many of the southwest's growers to look back into history and use what has always proved best for their particular terrain.

GRAPE VARIETIES
Arrufiat, Gros and Petit Manseng, Courbu

The Pacherenc wine can be tasted at the same address given for Madiran.

Whilst in the Madiran area, it would be a shame not to try the two nearby VDQS wines and make your comparisons, Tursan to the west and St-Mont to the east, all of them within a stone's throw of each other.

TURSAN VDQS

This is one of those regions where you begin to doubt yourself, for there is scarcely a vine to be seen on approaching from the south at least, but we can assure you there is plenty of wine. The area is worked by farmers, each of whom have a few vines, therefore there are no vast vineyards to see. Wine is red, white and rosé, but the one of chief interest is the white which comes to us via yet another local grape, the Baroque.

ADDRESS
Les Vignerons du Tursan, 40320 Geaune.
Friendly reception, busy place; the locals obviously appreciate the wines made here.

CÔTES DE ST-MONT VDQS

The origins of the St-Mont vineyard owe a lot to the Benedictine monks of St-Mont Abbey, and it is really an extension of the Madiran vineyard, this latter wine being one of its products as well as the VDQS reds, rosés and whites. The new grape here is the Colombard, used in the making of St-Mont's *vin de pays*, Côtes de Gascogne.

ADDRESS
Producteurs de Plaimont, 32400 Saint-Mont.
The staff at this union are very helpful, keen to spread the word about their wines. Variety of wine on offer.
The *route des vins de Madiran* is in this area to guide you around, but nearly all the St-Mont wine is at the Co-operative. An intriguing village sign announces that St-Mont is 'the village of manual therapy' and certainly it seems an industrious spot not only for wine, but for regional farm produce also.

IROULÉGUY

This last outpost of France, in Basque country, owes its presence entirely to the desire of a number of growers to continue the vine-growing tradition; yet another witness to the fact that the co-operative system has been the saving of not a few vineyards. But let's begin at the beginning. In the thirteenth century the monks of Roncevaux Abbey founded two priories in this land, one at Irouléguy, the other at Anhaux. The vine flourished until the monks were recalled to their monastery

Spotless whitewashed little houses and tiny parcels of vineyards make up the typical countryside at Irouléguy

following the treaty of the Pyrenees, after which the local families took over the work gladly. Phylloxera, world wars and a general rural exodus brought about a sad decline in Irouléguy's fortunes until a few growers got together to keep the tradition alive, resulting in a co-operative being formed and AC standard wine being achieved within no time.

GRAPE VARIETIES
Cabernet Franc
Cabernet Sauvignon
Tannat
Red wine and rosé is made here, the reds having the ability to age well especially after a good year, but also being pleasant to drink young.

ADDRESS
Cave Coopérative d'Irouléguy,
64430 Saint-Etienne-de-Baïgorry.
This is the sole source of Irouléguy wines, and it is immensely proud of them. A variety is offered and very little is seen outside the area.

A visit to this beautiful wine region would be a pleasure even had there not been any wine to discover. The countryside is dotted with spotless, whitewashed, little houses, immaculately kept, with the wooded foothills of the Pyrenees always in the background. People here like to keep up their traditions and the further away from the towns you roam, the more likely you are to see sights which would appear to belong to the last century. Long may it remain so!

LOCAL PRODUCTS AND SPECIALITIES
The Périgord is famous for its nuts and truffles, which account for much of those elusive flavours and aromas in its cuisine.

Confits (meats preserved in their fats), *foie gras*, dishes *farci* or stuffed, many of them using geese and poultry, are the things to try if you are spoiling yourselves.

Fruits, especially plums in the Agen region, and tomatoes at Marmande.

Madiran wine vies with the Gascon farm products surrounding it, making much use of poultry, geese and ducks.

Anything *à la béarnaise* will have a sauce of shallots and herbs with it, similar to the *paloise* sauce from Pau.

Mountain cheeses go without saying in the Pyrenees, a grand variety.

Basque dishes in the far south will be full of red peppers and will make use of local seafoods. Squid feature under the name of *chipiron*.

RECOMMENDED ROUTE
From Cahors follow the Lot to St-Cirq-Lapopie, cross the bridge there, return to Vers via the D662, head for Labastide-Murat via the D32. The D677 and D32 will take you to Rocamadour and from there aim for Lacave via the Ouysse valley. Souillac and the Dordogne take you to the wine region of Bergerac.

FURTHER INFORMATION
Comité Régional de Tourisme,
24, Allées de Tourny,
33000 Bordeaux.
For Cahors, Gaillac and Fronton:
Comité Régional de Tourisme,
BP2166,
12 rue Salambo,
31200 Toulouse.

GLOSSARY

Appellation d'Origine Contrôlée (AOC, AC)	controlled name of origin
blanc	white
bouteille	bottle
brut	dry (Champagne)
carte	wine list
cave	cellar
cépage	grape variety
chai	building for storing wine
chambré	at room temperature
chaptaliser	to chaptalise
château	wine estate
climat	individual vineyard, esp. in Burgundy
CM, coopérative/manipulant	Champagne co-operative
commune/finage	parish
coopérative	co-operative
crémant	sparkling wine
cru	growth
cuvée	a vatting or blending
dégustation	tasting
demi-sec	semi-sweet
domaine	wine estate
doux	sweet
edelzwicker (Ger.)	blend (in Alsace)
égrappoir	de-stalking machine
éleveur	one who matures wine, (as a *négociant*)
étiquette	label
expédition	export
ferme auberge	inn (in Alsace) with local food and drink
foire	fair
frais	chilled
grand cru	top rating for quality wine
gratuite	free
liquoreux	very sweet

liquoriste	liqueur maker
maître de chai	cellar master
marc	spirits
mas	wine estate in Provence
médaille (d'or, d'argent)	prize won at a wine competition
méthode champenoise	Champagne method for sparkling wine
millésime	year of wine
mis en bouteilles	bottled
moelleux	sweet
monopole	single ownership of a vineyard (Burgundy)
mousseux	sparkling
négociant (éleveur)	wine-merchant
NM, négociant/manipulant	Champagne *négociant*
nouveau	new wine, for early drinking
pays du vignoble	wine district
perlant	slightly sparkling
pétillant	another expression for slightly sparkling
pourriture noble	noble rot
premier cru	high rating for quality wine

Glossary

primeur	wine made very quickly for early drinking
propre récolte	wine from own produce
propriétaire	proprietor, owner
propriété	wine estate
RM, récoltant/manipulant	Champagne grower/producer
récolte	crop, harvest
rosé	pink wine
rouge	red wine
route de vin	vineyard-touring route
sec	dry wine
sentier (du vignoble)	footpath through vines
servir frais	serve chilled

spätlese (Ger.)	late harvest (Alsace), a sweeter wine
supérieur	slightly higher in alcohol
sur lie	on its lees (Muscadet)
tranquille	still wine
union viticole	wine co-operative
vendange	harvest
vendange tardive	late harvest, a sweeter wine
vente au détail	retail sales
vente directe	direct sales
vigneron	vineyard worker, usually the grower
villages	from chosen parishes in the region
vin de garde	wine for long keeping
vin délimité de qualité supérieure (VDQS)	delimited wine of superior quality
vin de paille	'straw' wine – Jura
vin de pays	country wine
vin de table	table wine, the lowest category
vin doux naturel (VDN)	fortified sweet wine
vin jaune	'yellow' wine – Jura
vin ordinaire	ordinary table wine
vins en vrac	'loose' wine, unbottled
viticulteur	wine grower
weinprobe (Ger.)	wine tasting, Alsace
weinstub (Ger.)	venue for wine tasting, Alsace

INDEX